"Dan shares decades of knowledge, and explains the most complex relationships of all, with skill and ease. The reader who has spent years trying to make sense of the most complex dyad of all, the borderline personality disorder (BPD) parent-adult child relationship, will not only find themselves in the pages but relate and identify with the outstanding lived-experience examples. This is a book that you will return to time and time again."

—**Fiona Yassin**, psychotherapist, founder of The Wave Clinic, and specialist in adolescent and family BPD

"Once again, Lobel offers hope and clarity to people navigating life within a bewildering and painful borderline system. Lobel's newest book brings his expertise and empathy into the reader's hands, opening a doorway to a healthier path forward. A must-read how-to guide for clinicians and clients alike."

—**Tracey Masella, LCW**, clinical director of the Krasner Adolescent Institute

"This book cleared up confusion about my relationship behavior that caused me pain for decades. The author's tone is warm and supportive, yet clear in pointing out hard truths I couldn't grasp until I saw them spelled out. Many of us with childhood trauma yearn for someone who understands. The author does. He'll show you how to heal and move on to freedom. Read this book—it will quickly improve your life."

—**Kristen Mancinelli, MS, RD**, author, and public health educator

"As a psychotherapist, researcher, and adult child of a borderline parent, Lobel's book has been invaluable in my own healing. It provides clear, step-by-step guidance on how to recognize, address, and heal the wounds resulting from being raised by a parent suffering from BPD. By taking a personal inventory of what was normalized that wasn't normal, I was able to take steps to emotionally reprocess past traumatic experiences with empowering results."

—**Nan Wise,** psychotherapist, certified sex therapist, certified
relationship specialist, behavioral neuroscience researcher
at Rutgers University, and author of *Why Good Sex Matters*

"Lobel is a master in his ability to distill what is regarded as one of the most complex and controversial diagnoses, into a concise and organized way. Those looking for a way to understand not only their parents with BPD, but also themselves, will benefit. This book will also serve as an important resource to clinicians in better understanding their work."

—**Kelly Krcmarik, MD**, attending psychiatrist, double-board
certified, Harvard- and Brown-trained

"Lobel has knocked it out of the park with this easy-to-read summary of borderline parents and their children. Lobel's clinical wisdom eases the reader through a comprehensive portrayal of the intergenerational implications of 'parenting while borderline'—a common but elusive clinical reality that gains clarity, and humanity, in Loebel's engaging depictions. This is a must-read for clinicians, adult children of borderline parents, and anyone who is curious about the science of emotional abuse and its sequelae."

—**Aaron Krasner, MD,** assistant professor of psychiatry at
Yale University, and CEO of the Krasner Adolescent Institute

Adult Children of Borderline Parents

A Trauma-Informed Guide to Recover from a Toxic Childhood & Discover a Healthy Sense of Self

Daniel S. Lobel, PhD

New Harbinger Publications, Inc.

NEW HARBINGER PUBLICATIONS is a registered trademark of New Harbinger Publications, Inc.

New Harbinger Publications is an employee-owned company.

Copyright © 2025 by Daniel S. Lobel, PhD
New Harbinger Publications, Inc.
5720 Shattuck Avenue
Oakland, CA 94609
www.newharbinger.com

Cover design by Amy Shoup

Acquired by Georgia Kolias

Edited by Diedre Hammons

Library of Congress Cataloging-in-Publication Data on file

Printed in the United States of America

27   26   25

10   9   8   7   6   5   4   3   2   1   First Printing

I would like to dedicate this book to all of you who have the courage to heal from being raised by a parent with symptoms of borderline personality disorder (BPD). Healing from any injury or illness is a challenge, but you have a special burden to overcome because of what you have experienced. For most of you, your childhood was devastated by a parent who was compromised by BPD, but chose to raise you anyway. Your family, to the extent that you have one, enabled your parent to raise you despite your parent's disability. Now, in order to heal and grow, you most likely have to go it alone. This is where your courage is tested.

Hopefully, you have support outside of the family. Ideally, this includes both professional help and loving support from friends and partners. Unfortunately, your parent and your family are likely to resist your efforts to heal and grow. They will likely see your setting boundaries as being mean or disrespectful to your parent, but it is necessary for your healing. It does not mean that your family doesn't love you—it just means they do not understand what you have been through and are going through. You can try to explain it to them, but be prepared to do what you have to do on your own. I laud your courageousness.

I would also like to dedicate this book to my wife, Diane, and my sons, Zachary and John. Without their technical and emotional support, you would not be reading these words. They are my rocks.

Contents

Introduction

Healing and Growth

Symptoms of borderline personality disorder (BPD) can have a profound effect on how parents raise their children. If you were raised by a parent with significant symptoms of BPD, then you may be suffering from the effects of their illness on your childhood and personal development. As you read on, you will come to understand things about yourself you were aware of but did not understand and discover aspects of yourself you didn't know existed.

You will also find some wounds you didn't know existed and understand better ones that you are aware of. Some of these wounds are traumatic. Common wounds are being the subject of your parent's aggression, such as when they lash out at you. Parental betrayal is another. This occurs when your parent turns against you and attacks you when your parent is displeased. Another is being intermittently or frequently gaslighted and lied to by a parent. Some of these wounds are associated with the tendency of parents with symptoms of BPD to discourage and inhibit their children's efforts to attain independence through personal growth. Other examples include isolating children from friends and other family members and attacking their self-confidence and self-esteem. Some of the wounds might not be traumatic but nonetheless have a significant effect on your past, present, and future.

If your parent has significant symptoms of BPD, this book is for you. Through this book, I will help you understand what has happened to you as a result of growing up under these conditions. I will give you the tools you need to heal your wounds and maximize your opportunities for personal growth.

Throughout this book, the accounts and experiences of others are provided for clarity and relatability. Those accounts and narratives labeled "ACOBP" are actual accounts by two individuals who grew up with a parent with symptoms of BPD. All other accounts and narratives are composed from my decades of clinical experience working with this population.

The challenge to recover from a childhood of trauma, emotional abuse, and mistreatment may seem formidable. Especially as you come to better understand the complexity of the processes of projection, gaslighting, and emotional instability, all of which are common under these circumstances.

Healing is a process—not an event. Relief will not come all at once. It will come incrementally as a result of your hard work, perseverance, and patience. You will be handsomely rewarded for your efforts. You will be able to take back most of what was taken from you and you will have the opportunity to be who you were meant to be. Who you want to be.

Who you deserve to be.

Part 1

Understanding Your Wounds— A Personal Inventory

Chapter 1

Growing Up with a Parent Suffering from BPD

Having a personality disorder in general, and borderline personality disorder (BPD) in particular, can profoundly affect the ways people behave in relationships. Intimate relationships are affected most because they are emotional. The relationship a person has with their child is one of the most intimate relationships any parent has and therefore most affected by the personality disorder. In this chapter, you will be offered a framework for understanding how your experience as the child of a person suffering from BPD is different from a healthy family experience and how this has affected you.

Normalizing That Which Is Not Normal

We enter the world genetically programmed to learn about the world through experience. Part of this programming is a tendency to egocentrically look at one's experience: children assume others experience what they experience and their experience is "normal." It is only much later in life, if at all, that young adults start to realize that everyone's experience is unique and therefore different.

Normal vs. Healthy

"Normal" is a statistical term that essentially means "that which is most common in a population." Natural tendencies toward conformity often lead to the assumption and belief that if most people do something, it must be healthy, but in many situations, this is not the case. For example, it is very common (normal) for people to overeat at buffets, but it is not healthy. Similarly, it is normal for people to avoid dealing with difficult or painful problems, but this practice is clearly not healthy. Throughout this book, the term "normal" will refer to what most people do. "Healthy" refers to what is recommended. In many instances, these will not correspond.

The developing child internalizes patterns of behavior within the family into their sense of how people should act toward each other. These patterns come to feel natural. In preschool children, family patterns are the primary ways children learn how to treat themselves and treat others. Ideally, children learn to be polite and have manners that become reflexive throughout their lifespan and guide healthy relationship functioning. Values such as respect for others, generosity, respect for laws and rules, community participation, and other positive values are introduced and reinforced through teaching and modeling.

Young children do not have the capacity to scrutinize their parents' behavior and identify patterns that are not normal. This is how unhealthy behavior patterns get passed down through the generations—and create core beliefs, which are actually myths—about what is normal. Some of these unhealthy behavior patterns associated with BPD are described below. As you read through the following descriptions, it may help you to reflect on your own experiences with your BPD parent and the false core beliefs that you may have internalized (or inherited).

Do as I Say, Not as I Do: The Power of Parental Modeling

In many families, parents teach (or in some cases, preach) certain values to their children, but do not follow their own teachings. They tell their children not to curse and raise their voices toward others, but when they are angry and frustrated, they curse and raise their voices. Often, this occurs around the children or even toward the children. Parents who smoke or drink excessively teach their children that this is unhealthy, but do it themselves. This produces a very confusing mixed message to the children. Certainly, parents violating their own teachings weaken their message. In most cases, modeling behavior is so much more powerful than verbal teachings that modeling neutralizes the verbal message altogether.

In addition to modeling unhealthy behaviors, parents can also provide a strong model for how the child is expected to react to the parent, even though the parent with symptoms of BPD may react differently. For example, parents with symptoms of BPD often model to their children that they have to accept aggressive lashing out, yet the parent does not tolerate the child lashing out at them. This type of non-reciprocal pattern is often present in the parenting behaviors of individuals with symptoms of BPD. Several examples are described below.

Myth: It Is Okay to Let Others Hurt You

Almost all parents, whether or not they have symptoms of BPD, tell their children it is not alright to let others hurt them. Lashing out aggressively at others, especially when frustrated, is a common symptom of BPD. Parents with these traits often lash out at their children with some frequency. When confronted about their lashing out, individuals with BPD are defensive and tend to explain or rationalize their aggressive behavior rather than condemn it. Here is an illustration.

Ari and Sheri's Story

Sheri, who has symptoms of BPD, is frustrated with her ten-year-old son, Ari, because she is late for an important meeting and she has to take Ari to school first.

Sheri: Ari, I need you to get out the door now and get to school.

Ari: I'll be right there.

Sheri: You said that twenty minutes ago.

Ari: I'm trying.

Sheri: Just get out the door.

Ari: Stop yelling at me.

Sheri: You little brat! You are lucky I don't smack you. I wish I never had a child!

Ari: Why are you hurting me?

Sheri: You are hurting me by making me late.

In the above example, Sheri was emotionally abusive to Ari because he was not able to get ready to leave fast enough for her, so she verbally lashed out at him and threatened to get physical. Ari had been told not to let others hurt him, but when he tried to stop his mother, she got more hurtful and then justified her abusive behavior.

Ari also observes his mother's behaviors toward others in the home when she is displeased. Ari has an infant sister named Teri. Mom is loving toward Teri most of the time. But one night, Ari heard Sheri yelling at Teri, who was having trouble sleeping and kept crying. Sheri looked very angry and even began shaking the baby while yelling at her to go to sleep. Fortunately, Ari's father came and took the baby and put her to sleep. Ari heard his mother telling his father that Teri wouldn't stop crying and she didn't know what else to do. Ari observed similar behavior between his mother and his father. His father did not like being treated this way, and sometimes protested, but he stayed married to her and continued to say that he loved her.

Ari never thought directly about the mixed messages he got about whether it was alright to let others hurt him, but both father and mother thought it was acceptable. Ari did not have difficulty making friends or finding girlfriends as he tended to be relatively passive and went along with what others wanted him to do. For example, some of Ari's friends and girlfriends were unkind to him when they did not get their way. They yelled at him or insulted him, but this did not strike him as unusual. Understandably, he attracted friends and lovers with strong personalities who liked to get their way.

Ari had no problem with this. It seemed "normal" to him because his friends' and girlfriends' behaviors were not nearly as offensive as what he experienced at home. Since he tolerates mistreatment, it gets worse. Ari has learned to be overly tolerant of mistreatment by others because he normalized mistreatment during childhood.

Myth: People Will Only Love You If You Please and Agree with Them

A core symptom of BPD is instability of mood, self-image, and relation-ships. This leads to a highly transactional quality to relationships—every encounter requires reiteration of allegiance and subordination. Failing to do so often results in rejection and sometimes retaliation through lashing out. Children of individuals with symptoms of BPD often develop a tendency to become *people pleasers*, people who persistently please others ahead of their own needs. Many people pleasers take extreme measures to be liked by others; they believe this is the only way they can maintain relationships.

In the previous example, Ari's mother makes it clear to her family that if you want to be loved by her, or even just to be safe with her, you have to continuously put her needs before yours. Ari grew up with this, so it became normal to him. When he was older, he rarely refused anyone's request regardless of how much sacrifice was required on his part.

Myth: Blame Others and Avoid Responsibility Whenever Possible

Since BPD is associated with a fragile sense of self, individuals suffering from symptoms of BPD often avoid taking blame when unwanted outcomes arise. They engage in *blame shifting*, blaming others for their errors. Blame shifting generally takes the form of arguing that any error they might have made was caused by something someone else did that "made them" do it.

Ray and Cal's Story

Ray, who suffers from symptoms of BPD, went out to dinner with his adult son, Cal. While they were eating, a storm developed outside. Even though Ray had driven them to the restaurant, Cal suggested he drive home: Ray had a few beers with dinner and Cal had only soft drinks. In addition, Ray recently had some vision problems and was soon to be evaluated for cataract surgery.

Ray refused to give Cal the car keys and was annoyed at Cal's suggestion that he might be impaired. Cal suggested Ray take sideroads rather than the highway, but Ray became even more annoyed and told Cal he didn't want his little boy to tell him what to do. On the way home, Ray hit a puddle and skidded off the road, colliding into a side rail. There was minor damage to the car, but no one was hurt. When they got home, they had the following conversation.

Cal: *Dad, I wish you had taken the sideroads.*

Ray: *It's your fault I skidded off the road!*

Cal: *My fault?*

Ray: *Yes. You made me so nervous with your worries, I was distracted.*

Cal wasn't surprised to hear this: it was consistent with how he was raised. He learned to do things himself, but because of his upbringing with a BPD parent, he emulated his father's behaviors in his adult life—he didn't have the opportunity to learn how to take responsibility with integrity when he made a mistake. For instance, when an error was found at work during an audit, he blamed the computer. When they checked the computer log, it was clear that there was no computer error. When they confronted Cal about making an error and lying about it, he blamed the auditor for targeting him and nitpicking. Had he taken responsibility for his error and agreed to be more careful, he would have kept his job. Instead, he was fired for lying about what happened.

Myth: Boundaries Are Offensive—And to Be Challenged

BPD is often described as a boundary disorder. This refers to difficulty or failure to understand the boundaries of others, resulting in violation of those boundaries. This is destructive to relationships. Healthy individuals respect the boundaries of others. They do not touch people who do not want to be touched. They do not enter places that have been forbidden. They do not press others for information or try to violate their privacy by trying to get cellphone or laptop passwords. They don't take things from others without asking first.

Many individuals with symptoms of BPD perceive the boundaries of others as a form of rejection. They are offended by the boundaries because they feel it means they are not trusted. The paranoia that is common in BPD often makes them feel they are being plotted against—and makes them want to violate these boundaries. They generally attempt to do this either directly or indirectly. Direct boundary violation is when it occurs overtly, deliberately, and sometimes defiantly. Acknowledgment of the breach is offered readily, sometimes followed by phrases such as, "If you don't like it, you can go f— yourself." Indirect challenges involve breaches that are not acknowledged as such.

Rex's Story

Rex, who has symptoms of BPD, rented a car for two days.
He signed a contract that stated that the car must be returned
by 12 p.m. or an additional day would be charged. He brought the
car back at 2 p.m. and was charged an additional day's rental.
He had the following conversation with the rental agent (RA):

Rex: *There is an error on the bill. You charged me for three*
               days, but I only had the car for two.

RA: *You returned the car late.*

Rex: *No, I didn't. I took the car on Monday and today*
               is Wednesday.

RA: *It says in the contract you have to return the car*
               by noon. It is after 2.

Ned: *You are going to charge me a whole day for two hours?*

RA: *It's in the contract.*

Rex:	*This isn't fair. How about we prorate it? I will give an extra $20.*
RA:	*It's not up to me. It is in the contract.*
Rex:	*Wow. You are terrible businesspeople. I will tell my friends to avoid your business.*

Rex challenged the noon boundary first through denial and then by arguing that the rule was unfair. When he still didn't get his way, he lashed out. When he got home, he shared this story with his son. He spoke proudly of giving the agent a "hard time" for imposing a silly and unfair penalty. He was teaching his son to view boundaries as offensive and to resist them. Do you recall getting confusing mixed messages from your parent or parents?

Individuals who suffer from symptoms of BPD often weaponize personal or private information that may have been expressed in a diary or to friends. They use it when it is convenient to do so to manipulate, humiliate, or guilt their children for thoughts or feelings. For example, Rob wanted his fifteen-year-old son, Ned, to help him with a home project. Ned was willing to help, but had plans at this particular time. They had the following conversation:

Ned and Rob's Story

Rob:	*Ned, I need you to help me this afternoon clean out the garage.*
Ned:	*I have plans this afternoon. Can we do it next week?*
Rob:	*I need it done now.*
Ned:	*I am sorry, I can't help you.*
Rob:	*I think it is in your interest to change your plans and help me.*

Ned: *What do you mean?*

Rob: *I mean if you don't, I will tell your mother what you said about her in your diary.*

Ned: *You read my diary?*

Rob: *The diary is in my house, so I am entitled to read it.*

Children raised by parents with symptoms of BPD often struggle with any sort of privacy. Their parent feels entitled to go through their children's rooms, drawers, homework, and electronic devices. The parents insist on access to their children's thoughts, feelings, dreams, and fears. As a result, children of individuals with symptoms of BPD become uncomfortable sharing any personal information with anyone. While they habitually avoid sharing such information, they also struggle to withhold such information when probed directly. During childhood, when they stated that they did not want to discuss a particular subject, they were probably punished. As adults, they fear making such statements and fear retaliation.

If your childhood experience included having your boundaries regularly challenged and violated by a parent, you may find that this interferes with intimacy with others. You may find that you do not feel comfortable sharing your feelings with friends and romantic partners and suffer anxiety when others try to get closer to you. This fear of sharing yourself with others often strains and sometimes completely undermines efforts to share a life with someone who loves you.

The Pain You Feel but Cannot Find

Above are descriptions of just some of the types of beliefs and experiences you may have normalized growing up in a family with a parent with symptoms of BPD that are not normal or healthy. The feelings and reactions associated with these beliefs can be very difficult to identify because they are woven deeply into your personality as the result of repeated exposure to behaviors that support these beliefs. These beliefs were associated with severe punishment if you did not comply or adhere. Tragically, it can be a sort of indoctrination or brainwashing that when done in childhood becomes very difficult to discern from the experience of the self. These are beliefs and reactions that have come to feel very natural and automatic. These programmed reactions can cause significant and pervasive suffering to those raised under these circumstances. These reactions are difficult to find the root of and hence difficult to cope with. Following are some common examples of the kinds of programmed reactions that may be unconsciously driving your own behavior and causing you to suffer.

Chronic Feelings of Guilt

Most children of individuals with symptoms of BPD report intense and persistent feelings of guilt. When asked what they feel guilty about, they are unable to articulate a clear answer. They indicate they know they haven't done anything wrong, but feel guilty nonetheless. This creates a dark cloud over their lives, especially during joyful times.

A common experience is that these individuals grew up in an environment where they were persistently told that their efforts were insufficient and they were punished for being "not good enough." Individuals with symptoms of BPD send this message to those who try to get close to them persistently for two reasons. One reason is that the requests or demands of these individuals are more symbolic than facilitative. For example, a parent asks the child to clean their room or provide a ride to the store and then finds some reason to complain upon completion of the task. It wasn't done quickly enough, clean enough, or with the proper attitude. The child is left wondering why they're being punished for compliance. The problem is, to the parent, the task is symbolic of the child's willingness to be infinitely accessible and compliant. In doing so, this makes the parent feel safe, supported, and loved. This symbolic request is not appropriate from a parent to a child and is thereby not achievable. Even children who pursue every opportunity to reassure their parent will eventually fail, not because the child's performance is insufficient, but because the parent is looking for emotional caretaking from the child that the parent can only get from themselves, but they don't know how. Therefore, the parent is chronically unsatisfied and generally unencumbered in expressing this dissatisfaction to others.

The second reason parents with symptoms of BPD often make their loved ones feel guilty is that it serves as a form of blame shifting. Most individuals with symptoms of BPD are fearful of taking responsibility for errors or unwanted outcomes because it makes them feel flawed and unlovable. This is why blame shifting is very common among people with this disorder. They often claim to be the victim and everyone else is to blame. This is often made explicitly clear whenever possible.

Being told persistently that you are not good enough and frequently blamed for things that are beyond your control during childhood often causes chronic feelings of guilt that can linger across the lifespan. This probably causes you to meticulously avoid errors and to experience anxiety when required to perform. Even if you are not aware of doing anything wrong, you worry you will be blamed anyway. At the very least, this will prevent you from performing comfortably. At moderate levels, the anxiety associated with the guilt can inhibit optimal performance. At high levels of anxiety, your physical and mental health may be compromised.

Fear of "Rocking the Boat"

Households with parents with symptoms of BPD often have a lot of drama. The instability of mood, self-image, and relationships that most parents with symptoms experience is associated with unstable and impulsive behavior. This is often driven more by strong emotion than careful thought. The result is frequent and sometimes intense conflicts where strong emotion is expressed in an unkind way. This produces a persistent atmosphere of drama.

A child being raised in this type of environment learns to avoid conflict and drama as much as possible. Some try to first join in the drama, but eventually learn that drama is about the parent or parents with BPD symptoms and the child is at an insurmountable disadvantage. Eventually, they start to manifest symptoms of stress or depression and then they learn avoidance.

This type of avoidance is sometimes referred to as "walking on eggshells." This involves conducting interactions with a primary goal of avoiding conflicts or even emotional escalation rather than communication or problem solving. Interactions, topics, or events may be avoided if they have previously been shown to involve conflict.

If you grew up in an environment like this, you probably avoid all types of conflict, even outside of the family. When you are confronted or drawn into a conflict or disagreement, you probably experience very high levels of anxiety. Many experience anxiety to such a high level they become paralyzed during conversations that are at all emotional. This reaction can be so powerful, they cannot think of any response. They often think of appropriate responses after the interaction has ended, when it is too late to be effective.

Chronic Feelings of Isolation

There are numerous aspects of growing up with a parent with symptoms of BPD that leave you feeling isolated. Some of the most common are discussed below.

Damaged Trust

The unstable mood and behavior common to many parents suffering from symptoms of BPD undermine the trust of those who depend on them. Children of affected parents at times experience a parent who is loving and cooperative; at other times, they experience the same parent as aggressive, agitated, and in some cases, abusive. These different ways of relating to the children are largely determined by that parent's emotions and mood at any given moment. At any time, the parent can be in an aggressive/agitated state without provocation. Even when the parent is in the loving/cooperative modality, they can quickly revert to aggressive/agitated and therefore cannot be emotionally trusted to be available, supportive, or even competent as a parent. The child can sometimes get some needs met by the parent, yet there is no consistency and hence no reliability. They cannot trust the parent at any given time to have a reasonable and cooperative demeanor, so these children quickly learn to go elsewhere to have their needs met. Bottom line, they do not trust their parent to be there for them. If you can't trust your parent, it is almost impossible to trust anyone else.

Lying, Gaslighting, and Blame Shifting

Individuals with symptoms of BPD often lie, gaslight, and blame shift with their children as they avoid responsibility for errors and unwanted outcomes. The child quickly learns that although sometimes the parent is truthful, the parent frequently relies on dishonesty to protect their unstable sense of self. Every single time the child becomes aware of the parent lying, it is a lesson to the child not to trust others.

Lying, gaslighting, and blame shifting are also forms of betrayal. Young children are completely dependent on adults to take care of them. When the parent sacrifices the well-being of the child to protect their own ego, the child experiences a sense of loneliness and abandonment that shakes their world every time. Here is what happened to Sherman.

Sherman's Story

Sherman was six years old when his father moved out and left him with his mother, who had symptoms of BPD. Sherman was very attached to his father and was crestfallen when he learned of his father's leaving. He begged his father to stay. His father promised he would call every day and see him every weekend.

The first week, Sherman's father called every day and they spoke. This gave him some level of stability and security as his household was torn apart. One day, Sherman came in from playing with friends and asked his mother if Dad had called. She said that he hadn't, but perhaps would call later. Sherman did not speak to his father that day.

Sherman did not speak to his father for several days. He kept asking his mother if his father had called and his mother said no. He asked his mother why Dad stopped calling and his mother said, "I guess it's not important to him. Maybe he stopped loving you." Sherman was crushed. He believed his mother and felt betrayed by his father. One day, the phone rang while Mom was in the bathroom. Generally, Sherman was not permitted to answer the phone, but this time, he did. It was his father! Sherman was stunned. They had the following conversation:

Sherman: *Dad, why haven't you been calling like you said you would?*

Dad: *I have been.*

Sherman: *Why didn't you talk to me?*

Dad: *Your mother kept hanging up on me and telling me you didn't want to talk to me.*

Sherman: *I thought you didn't love me anymore.*

Dad: *That will never happen.*

After the conversation with his father, Sherman fearfully confronted his mother in a way he had not done before. His mother justified her behavior by stating she was punishing his father for not paying child support. Sherman couldn't believe it. The only two people he had to take care of him, and protect him, both disappeared at the same time. He was lied to—and betrayed. He knew he would never trust his mother ever again and wasn't sure if he could ever trust anybody.

Secure attachment is based on consistency. When people treat each other with respect over time and circumstances, such treatment becomes anticipated. The more these anticipations are met, the more safe people feel and the relationship becomes progressively more secure. Without trust, secure attachment is impossible. An in-depth discussion of how attachment patterns affect children of parents with symptoms of BPD is in chapter 4. The absence of secure attachment combined with damaged trust and betrayal of primary attachment figures leaves children of individuals with symptoms of BPD feeling alone even when they are with others. Especially when they are with their parents.

In this chapter, you learned about some patterns of behavior that are common in households of parents with symptoms of BPD. If you grew up in such a household, you are likely to have come to believe these patterns are normal. Since you believed these patterns to be normal, you developed wounds you could not see. The cause of these wounds was thought to be invalid because the behaviors that caused them were considered to be normal. In the next chapter, we will look at the traumatic experiences that many children of people who suffer from symptoms of BPD endure and the traumatic wounds that arise. The second section of this book is devoted to healing these wounds, but first, you have to recognize them.

Chapter 2

Traumatic Experiences During Formative Years

As you read the following chapter, you may find references to experiences similar to your own that you never thought of as being traumatic. This is because when you and others in your household are regularly exposed to treatment others might find traumatic, the treatment becomes normalized and no longer feels out of the ordinary. Be prepared to reevaluate some past experiences as you explore whether you will allow such treatment in the future. Understanding past experiences from a different perspective—emotional reprocessing—is a core part of your healing process, which will be discussed in chapter 7.

Trauma is defined as an experience with "exposure to actual or threatened death, serious injury, or sexual violence."[*] Individuals who are raised by parents with BPD are likely to experience trauma in their early lives because of the instability and impulsivity characteristic of BPD. This causes parents to respond erratically to many situations and is often affected by compromised judgment and inappropriate behavior. For example, over time, children might get used to their parent getting

---

[*]   American Psychiatric Association (APA). 2013. Diagnostic and Statistical Manual of Mental Disorders, 5th ed. Arlington, VA: American Psychiatric Publishing.

into shouting matches with strangers, vendors, friends, and family when the parent does not get their way. The child comes to expect this. In addition, children raised by parents with BPD are regularly exposed to trauma that is rarely found in households with stable parents. People who suffer from symptoms of BPD can exhibit sexually, mentally, physically, and emotionally self-destructive behavior. Watching a parent intentionally cut or burn themselves is a common example. This we will refer to as *non-targeted* trauma because the child is not the target of the parent's behavior—just a bystander.

Most prominent in this category is the psychological trauma the child experiences when the child is the target of the parent's manipulation or abuse, or *targeted trauma*. This is almost certainly the most destructive aspect of being raised by a parent with BPD and will be described in detail and with examples below.

Non-Targeted Trauma

Parents with symptoms of BPD frequently manifest socially disruptive behaviors. When they do this in the presence of their children, the children may be traumatized by these behaviors and the reactions of others to these behaviors. Individuals with BPD often suffer from impulsivity, which interferes with their ability to think things through before choosing actions, and behavior that reflects poor judgment. This is also generally associated with emotional dysregulation. Lashing out when frustrated, challenged, or displeased is a very common behavior. Ann's story is an illustration of this.

Ann's Story

Even as a child, Ann did not like to go to public places with her mother. She knew it was uncomfortable in ways she did not feel when she was with other adults, but didn't have a clear understanding of why, so she avoided it whenever possible. As she entered her teenage years, she began to recognize a pattern where her mother would say mean things to others whenever she was displeased by them or displeased in general. One time, they came out of a store together and a parking enforcement employee was ticketing the car. Her mother approached the person and demanded the ticket be torn up. When the parking enforcement person refused to comply, her mother angrily tore the ticket up and started shouting profanities. Naturally, the officer called the police for backup and a scene ensued. Ann was so embarrassed, she hid her face for fear she be recognized by peers. She was so upset by the event, she couldn't sleep that night.

Ann lived alone with her mother; her parents separated when she was three years old. They lived in a small apartment due to limited financial resources. Ann often awoke in the middle of the night to find her mother entertaining men in the living room. Throughout her childhood, she saw many different men with her mother, none of whom were introduced to her. They would come after she was in bed and leave before morning. She would find empty liquor glasses and bottles in the morning and occasionally wrappers from condoms or spermicide in the bathroom. She generally returned to bed quietly without allowing her mother to know that she had woken up.

One night, she heard her mother groaning in a way that sounded like her mother could be hurt. She cracked her door and saw her mother and a man without clothing. She knew what was happening. She went back to her room and closed her eyes in an effort to return to sleep. Then she heard her mother scream out in pain. She got up to see what was happening and saw her mother screaming at the man as he ran toward the door. Her mother was holding a kitchen knife and she had blood on her leg. When Ann asked what was happening, her mother told her everything was *alright and to go back to sleep. She was terrified. Ann struggled with falling asleep for the rest of her childhood as she did not feel safe in the apartment.*

Ann was also troubled by seeing her mother involved in self-destructive acts when agitated. Her mother frequently cut, bit, or burned herself when she was upset. Ann's mother had numerous wounds and scars on her arms and legs that were self-inflicted. Around others, she wore long sleeves and pants that covered these wounds and scars, but at home, Ann could see these wounds all the time. On occasion, she actually saw her mother self-mutilate. This both puzzled her and terrified her.

Targeted Trauma

This is mistreatment or abuse that many children of parents with BPD experience when the parent is displeased with them. One very common form is frequent screaming at the child. This often includes insults, expletives, and threats. This less commonly occurs in public, so the child is isolated and trapped. The parent often continues until the child is in a state of rage or panic. Commonly, threatening behavior by the parent with BPD does not involve direct assault of the child; however, their behavior suggests that it could happen. The parent adopts a rageful posture, facial expression, and vocal tone while hitting objects, breaking objects, or hitting or kicking walls. Often, the aggression is targeted at coveted items of the child.

The threatening behavior of the parent also often includes physically acting out. This might include direct assault on the child while in a rageful state. In extreme cases, this might threaten the child's survival. Shaken baby syndrome is an example where the parent gets frustrated or angry with an infant and violently shakes them. Because of the delicate skeletal structure of infants' heads and the fragile developing brain, permanent brain damage or death is often the result.

Another form of targeted aggression toward the child is the parent mutilating themselves in front of the child, often blaming the child for the parent's self-mutilation. For example, Roddy's father often ended arguments with him by punching a hole in the wall in Roddy's room. He would then show Roddy his bloody hand and say, "You see what you made me do? You are a rotten, ungrateful child!"

In Roddy's example, the traumatic aspect of the encounter comes not only from the implied physical threat to Roddy but also from his father gaslighting him: making him feel guilty/wrong/crazy for making/forcing his father to hurt himself and destroy property. This was then followed by a vitriolic rant about what a terrible son Roddy is for disagreeing. The attack on Roddy's character and self-worth makes the abusive behavior much more traumatic. Childhood is when critical aspects of the self are formed and formulated—this is when people begin the lifelong process of discovering who they are. These attacks on character at this developmental phase by a parent undermine the child's development of a stable sense of self and are likely to result in anxiety and other debilitating symptoms throughout the lifespan—if not healed.

Good and adequate parents can on occasion get frustrated or angry at their child and raise their voice, say something unkind, or even slam a door in anger. But healthy parents reflect on their behavior and apologize to the child. Individuals with BPD are generally loathe to take responsibility for something they did wrong and hence unlikely to apologize. Rather, they are more likely to blame the child. "Gaslighting" is when the parent lies about something and then makes the child feel either crazy, stupid, or wrong for not agreeing with the lie, like when Roddy's father lied about the cause of putting his hand through the wall and then making Roddy feel bad about himself so that he would not challenge the fabrication.

The trauma of realizing that your parent, who you are largely or totally dependent on, will betray you whenever you do not agree with them is almost exclusively found in parents suffering from BPD and some narcissistic traits. It is imperative to your healing that you understand this type of trauma as it can profoundly affect your ability to have intimate relationships with others.

Other forms of parental betrayal trauma include public humiliation, character assassination, and polarization.

Public Humiliation

Parents with symptoms of BPD sometimes shame or humiliate others to elevate themselves in the eyes of others who are present. It is a form of bullying, like you would see in elementary or middle school, and hence regressive behavior.

The traumatic impact on the children of these parents is compounded by their vulnerability toward shaming associated with the natural instability of a developing sense of self. This is an attack on the child's self-esteem and self-confidence at a time in life when the child needs accurate feedback and support. In addition, public humiliation is another form of parental betrayal. It also makes the child feel awkward and uncomfortable around whoever witnessed the shaming.

For example, Roddy's father goes fishing with his two brothers once a year. When Roddy turned fourteen, his father offered to bring him along. He enjoyed being around his uncles and loved fishing, but he did not like his father's frequent recounting of stories that put him in a bad light. For example, his father loved to tell stories about his getting carsick on trips and throwing up all over the car.

When Roddy was fifteen, his father asked him again to go fishing with his uncles. Roddy told his father that he enjoyed the fishing and company, but did not like being made fun of. He and his father had the following exchange:

Dad: *It's not my fault you are a weakling and can't take it.*

Rod: *If that's the way you feel, I think I will stay home.*

Dad: *Your choice.*

Rod: *Are you saying that you will not stop shaming me?*

Dad: *Okay, okay. I will be careful.*

On the way to meet his uncles, Roddy reminded his father that he had committed to not shaming him during this trip. His father nodded his head. Roddy was particularly concerned about his father potentially mentioning a very embarrassing situation that occurred between Roddy and his sister's friend that was very painful for him. He wanted to tell his father especially not to bring up the incident, but he was also worried that reminding his father might make it more likely that he would talk about it.

The second evening of the trip, his father brought it up in the most humiliating way imaginable. One of the uncles was telling a story about a man at work who was humiliated by a woman he was attracted to. Roddy's father chuckled and then said, "Roddy would know." Of course, one uncle asked Roddy what his father meant. Roddy was immediately put in the humiliating situation of having to recount an embarrassing story or decline to do so. He declined and was quiet for the rest of the trip. When they were riding home after the trip, Roddy and his father had the following conversation:

Rod: *Dad, I asked you not to humiliate me in front of your brothers.*

Dad: *I didn't say anything.*

Rod: *You set me up.*

Dad: *I told you before—you are just too sensitive.*

Roddy realized at that point that he could not trust his own father. That his father would betray him whenever it benefits his father to do so and then gaslight him when he tries to discuss it with him. Roddy also was no longer comfortable in front of his uncles because his father shamed him, so he rarely sees or talks to them anymore.

The traumatic impact for Roddy is not just from the single shaming event. The full impact comes from the realization that his primary support and attachment—his parent—is willing to betray him whenever it is expedient to do so. Repeated experiences like this throughout childhood cause a profound sense of isolation and trauma-level avoidance of trusting others. When children regularly experience these types of betrayal with a parent throughout childhood, it encourages the belief that other people in general are not trustworthy and that it is not safe to trust them.

Character Assassination

The instability of the sense of self combined with the tendency to think about things in black-and-white terms encourage individuals with BPD to see others as either good or bad. The transactional nature that comes with their unstable sense of self makes them believe they can decide whether others are good or bad. When others disagree with them or are otherwise seen as a threat, they make a case for them as being bad people, which allows them to marginalize or dismiss the opinions, feelings, and needs of others.

So, when parents with BPD feel threatened by their child, they often assassinate the child's character. This often involves calling them names such as "loser" or "piece of crap." It also manifests in them attacking the self-worth of the child, such as:

"You are ungrateful."

"I wish you were never born."

"I would have been better off without you."

"You are ruining my life."

Being spoken to this way by a parent is devastating for a child trying to figure out who they are and consolidate their sense of self. As the child gets older, they notice that the parent speaks to them differently when they are pleased or not threatened. The parent may even compliment or idealize the child if they comply. This type of treatment encourages the child to become a people pleaser. They learn to put pleasing others ahead of their own needs to avoid being disparaged or abused.

Children of parents with BPD bring the people pleasing into other intimate relationships in their lives. They believe that they must please others to avoid being mistreated or abused and to be liked or accepted. This reinforces their weak self-esteem by always putting others first. They also often develop resentment toward those that they are pleasing, much as they feel toward the parent that forced them to do so, which undermines the relationship. In this way, they recreate the relationship they had with the parent with BPD with every other object of their affection. In chapter 9, you will learn how to have relationships that do not involve people pleasing and are more stable and satisfying than those you have in your life thus far.

Polarization

Most individuals suffering from symptoms of BPD have a profound fear of abandonment and being alone. As a result, they are preoccupied with seeking attention, affection, and loyalty from others. Those they seek attention and affection from become isolated from other important people in their lives through competition and triangulation.

The competition often manifests as character assassination of their children's friends or other associates. They see friends of their child, and later partners or spouses of their child, as a threat to their access to their child. They may even see their own grandchild as a threat. For this reason, they often seek to disparage friends and lovers. When conflicts do come up, they triangulate, reconceptualizing events so that it forces the child to have to choose between the parent and a friend or another relative.

Ann's Story

Ann's mother put her in this position over and over again. For example, Ann had made plans to meet with her friend Sunday afternoon. They were going to meet for lunch, meet some school friends, and go to a high school football game. On Saturday, her mother asked her to be available on Sunday to take her to get a manicure. She liked to be driven to the appointment so she wouldn't have to worry about smearing her nail polish if it was still wet.

Mom: *Ann, I need you to take me tomorrow for my nail appointment at noon.*

Ann: *I am sorry, but I have plans with my friends tomorrow at that time.*

Mom: *Which friends?*

Ann: *Jean, and later, a few others from school.*

Mom: *You choose that little tramp over me. Some way to treat your mother.*

Ann: *I didn't know you had a nail appointment when I made plans with my friends.*

Mom: *Can't you meet your friends after my appointment?*

Ann: *No. We are going to a football game.*

Mom: *You choose your friends and football over me! I guess I mean nothing to you.*

Ann: *Why don't you change your appointment to a time when I don't have plans?*

Mom: *Never mind. Now that I know what an ungrateful piece of dirt you are, I would rather go alone.*

Ann's mother managed to triangulate both her friend Jean and football. When Ann refused to change her plans, her mother used character assassination to punish her. Ann felt good that she did not give in to her mother, as she might have when she was younger, but she did not enjoy the outing because she could not stop thinking about the conflict with her mother and how hurtful her mother was when she did not get her way.

It wasn't until much later in adult life that Ann and Roddy fully experienced the impact of the realization that the aggression and ruthlessness they saw their parent direct toward others was also directed toward them. You might be going through this as you read this chapter. If so, have faith that the pain you are allowing yourself to feel is the first step toward healing and growth. The remaining chapters in this book will guide you to reclaiming your life and yourself. In the next section, you will see how these experiences have resulted in trauma symptoms that you may have not identified as such but affect you daily nonetheless.

General Trauma Symptoms

The following are symptoms that commonly appear following exposure to most traumatic experiences.

Intrusive recollections are memories of past traumatic events that suddenly enter your awareness, often in an unwanted form. Nightmares are common forms. Victims of trauma also often experience flashbacks, when memories or parts of memories from past events intrude into awareness. Nightmares tend to be largely visual, although somatic intrusions are not unusual. Examples of somatic intrusions can include paralysis, experiencing distracting sounds that occurred during the initial trauma, and feeling cold or hot. Regardless of the form they appear, intrusive recollections are often distortions of what actually occurred. They might involve different people or surroundings. Some intrusive recollections might be of small parts of the memory, such as imagining certain scents or having feelings of being trapped or panic.

Avoidance following reminders of the traumatic event(s) is extremely common. For example, near-death experiences in airplanes or boats can result in phobias and avoidance of these activities, environments, and even themes. This is how traumatic triggers are formed. Individuals who have survived traumatic or abusive childhoods often avoid their relatives, childhood homes, and other aspects of daily life that remind them of that time. In some cases, they avoid intimate relationships—or relationships altogether.

Panic attacks are common among trauma survivors. Nightmares and flashbacks are often accompanied by significant anxiety, which can occur during the flashback or immediately after. It is not uncommon for people to wake from nightmares in a cold sweat and a panic state.

Dissociation is experienced as feeling numb and a sense that things are not real (derealization). It is sometimes described as watching oneself on television, or as if the self is not real. These dissociated periods are often followed by amnesia for events that occur during these episodes. Some people lose the ability to account for minutes, hours, or even days during these periods. Individuals experiencing childhood trauma often learn to induce these periods when they perceive they are in a traumatic situation they cannot escape from. Dissociation allows them to escape in their minds, but unfortunately, the body is left to endure. This can also manifest as people having injuries, but being unable to account for the cause. Dissociation, which was crafted as a coping mechanism in childhood during traumatic events, often becomes automatic. These states are no longer consciously induced but rather they occur automatically during stress or discomfort. Part of your healing will involve taking control of this mechanism. You will learn how to do this in the coming chapters.

Trauma Symptoms Associated with Growing Up with a Parent with BPD

The following symptoms are specific to exposure to parental trauma. These symptoms occur most commonly in individuals who are raised by a parent with a severe personality disorder.

Experiencing discomfort/anxiety around adults is the result of persistent intimidation from a parent. The impulsivity and emotional dysregulation experienced by most sufferers of BPD result in frequent lashing out at others, including their children. If your entire childhood experience involved being the subject of parental rage, you will very likely fear adults and authority figures throughout your life.

In addition to the discomfort children of parents with BPD often experience, many find themselves compromised in their functioning around adults and authority figures. For many, their fear and anxiety are distracting and interfere with clarity of thought. For some, flashbacks may occur, resulting in panic attacks and temporary paralysis.

Difficulty trusting others is a direct result of being betrayed and gaslighted by the person you had to trust the most: your parent. If you cannot trust your parents, who can you trust? Trust occurs as a result of feeling safe with others. Many survivors of childhood with a BPD parent never feel safe with others. An important part of your healing and growth will require that you learn to create safety in relationships.

Excessive defensiveness is the natural reaction to growing up feeling attacked much of the time. Individuals with symptoms of BPD often avoid taking responsibility for errors or unwanted outcomes, which results in blaming others when things don't go their way. Parents with BPD often make statements like "I wish you were never born" to their children when angry or frustrated. This is a sweeping blame shift of their entire lives onto the child. One parent, for example, blamed her child for having an episiotomy (a common minor surgical procedure to facilitate vaginal delivery). Frequent exposure to these attacks encourages the child to be defensive. The lashing out common in BPD is often rageful and the child becomes so intimidated that they avoid taking responsibility even when they make a minor error. These children often become habitually defensive. For many, this defensiveness can compromise intimate relationships. How to identify and heal from this wound will be discussed in chapter 4.

Feeling an excessive need to justify is a reaction to being raised by a parent who views relationships as transactional. The instability of mood, behavior, and relationships that is characteristic of BPD interferes with them seeing others in the context of past experience and behavior. Rather, they see each interaction with others as a new relationship. They require others to justify their wants, needs, and requests over and over again—you are compelled to justify your feelings, preferences, requests, etc. each time you transact. For example, after a history of lying and gaslighting, they still ask you why you don't trust them. Throughout childhood, individuals with parents with BPD expect to have to justify their feelings, preferences, and requests so they do so in advance. This becomes habitual and is done in all or most relationships and can lead to a tendency to overshare in relationships, which can be a disadvantage in many situations. A common example is justifying why they cannot agree to meet others. When asked, "Can you meet Tuesday at noon?" they respond, "I cannot meet then *because I have a dentist's appointment.*" Offering an excuse for not meeting at a particular time conveys that it is alright to scrutinize why you can't make it. This suggests that your judgment is not sufficient, so you overshare it with others because theirs is more valid. This is disrespectful to yourself and weakens your self-esteem.

In this chapter, we considered the types of traumatic exposure you might have experienced in childhood if you were raised by a parent with BPD. With the use of illustrations, we explored the short-term effects on you of being treated this way by your parent—the person you depended on most. In the next two chapters, we will look at the long-term effects of your repeated exposure to these types of mistreatment throughout your childhood and into adulthood and how to heal these wounds and grow into the person you were meant to be with the love in your life you deserve to have.

Chapter 3

Damage to Your Developing Self

Optimization of your quest for healing and growth will require you to understand your traumatic and unstable childhood from a child's perspective. The damaging effects of persistent exposure to the typical behaviors of an emotionally dysregulated parent are multiplied exponentially when meted out on young children. This is because children have not yet fully developed their personality, which makes them particularly vulnerable to damage to the emerging self.

What Is a Self and How Does It Get Damaged?

Your concept of who you are is defined by a combination of thinking, feeling, and behavior patterns. These patterns of behavior are based on genetics and experience. Paranoia, for example, is a pattern of suspicious thinking that looks at others as being evil or conspiratorial. This pattern of thinking often develops after multiple experiences of victimization by others, such as being the subject of bullying or discrimination.

A pattern of feeling or emotion is the way you experience the world around you. Congenital differences cause us to perceive the world around us differently, which is why some people prefer vanilla to chocolate, or warm climates to cold ones. These preferences are often based on minor variations in the way each individual's nervous system is wired, but experience often plays a critical role. Acquired tastes for certain foods or beverages is an example of how experience may alter how someone's taste wiring may change.

A traumatic experience can affect feelings about aspects of the world around you in a very significant way. When individuals experience a traumatic event (or series of events), all aspects of the environment can become "triggers" of intrusive recollections about these events. For example, a bad auto accident on a particular interstate can cause you to experience fear when in cars, when driving on that same interstate, or anything else that might be associated with the crash. If the crash occurred in the rain, it can produce a fear response to driving in the rain on future trips. Experiences such as these can affect the way you perceive these triggers for the rest of your life.

Behavior patterns are the ways people respond to different events and conditions. We are born with instinctive behavior patterns, such as reflexes. These are responses to events such as pain, feeling like we are off-balance, or a drop in temperature, that occur automatically: the responses require little or no thought. Other patterns of behavior are created by contingency: patterns of reward and punishment. We tend to repeat behaviors we are rewarded for and avoid behaviors that bring punishment.

From these patterns of thinking, feeling, and behavior come personality traits. Again, patterns of responses become generalized and automatic. Examples of personality traits include being suspicious, avoidant, angry, impatient, compassionate, or generous. The more consistent a person is in utilizing character traits across situations, the more stable the personality becomes. Stability is associated with less anxiety while unstable personalities suffer more.

The human brain requires over twenty years after a healthy gestation to fully develop. As the brain develops, the ability for more complex understanding—the ability to conceptualize the self—is enhanced. As you get older, your brain becomes more able to compare information from different sources, even if that information is in conflict. Young children do not have this ability, which makes them more susceptible to the effects of trauma and mistreatment.

The core symptom of BPD is instability in mood, self-concept, and behavior associated with unstable relationships. Development of a stable sense of self is facilitated by a stable parenting environment. This involves consistent treatment and feedback to the child in a loving context. Parents with significant BPD symptoms struggle to be stable parents. The remainder of this chapter will focus on understanding the damage done to you by your parent's instability. There are three ways that symptoms of BPD can damage their child's developing sense of self.

Inhibition of Growth

A very common symptom of BPD is fear of abandonment. When the parent experiences this to a significant extent, they become invested in keeping you accessible. This is not consistent with encouraging growth and hence independence. This is a form of codependency, where the parent encourages you to remain dependent by discouraging growth.

This can take many different forms. A common form is that the parent is overcontrolling. The parent makes all decisions for the child and discourages the child from taking charge of his or her life. Rather than explaining why decisions are made, they respond, "Because I said so." This inhibits the child from developing judgment and decision making-skills while keeping the child dependent on the parent's permission.

Another form of inhibition of growth can come from the parent discouraging or prohibiting activities that enhance development such as peer events, afterschool events, summer camp, boarding school, etc. They sometimes discourage sleepovers at other children's homes. They often put geographical limits on college if boarding is considered at all.

A more damaging but very common form of inhibition is discouraging the development of opinions or preferences that are different from the parent's. Your interests or opinions that differ from your parent's are seen as threatening to their ability to secure access to you. These interests or opinions are often discouraged, ridiculed, and frequently attacked. Roddy had this problem with his father.

Roddy's Story

After his father shamed him while fishing with his uncles, Roddy stopped going fishing. He didn't have anyone else to go with and he did not enjoy going with his father. A number of Roddy's friends became involved with social media, and soon, he got involved too. He tried to share it with his father, but his father was uninterested and stated, "I don't waste my time with that stuff."

Following that conversation, his father went on a campaign to discourage Roddy from participating in social media with his friends. This included attacks on those friends. That weekend, Roddy and his father had the following conversation.

Dad: *Roddy, I need you to help me on Sunday to repair the light fixture in the bathroom.*

Rod: *I have plans on Sunday. Can we do it on Saturday?*

Dad: *What? Are you going to make TikToks with those losers you call friends?*

Rod: *We are not using TikTok. We are making a website. We hope to make some money.*

Dad: *Like when you were five and you wanted to make money selling lemonade?*

Many adolescents would continue this project with their friends and not share it with their fathers. But for Roddy, this part of himself was already damaged. When he was seven, he wanted to join the Cub Scouts, but his father ridiculed him because they were "fake soldiers." His mother advocated for him and his father gave in, but somehow, his father was late registering and he missed out. In fourth grade, he wanted to join a dance club at school, but his father wouldn't sign the permission slip because "dancing is for girls."

The part of Roddy that is adventurous and seeks new experiences and diverse social experiences was stymied. He experienced self-doubt and anxiety in new situations and when his father shot down his efforts, he simply relented. He no longer had the confidence to pursue anything that his father did not endorse. His natural desire to grow had been damaged and his enthusiasm was replaced with fear and dread of his father's criticism and discouragement. He lost confidence in himself and his choices and became fearful of new directions. His growth was effectively stunted.

Contamination of Self

Contamination, sometimes referred to as "brainwashing," occurs when perceptions, thoughts, beliefs, or feelings are inserted into awareness by others in such a way that they are mistaken for one's own perceptions, beliefs, or feelings. The developing self is particularly vulnerable to contamination during childhood because it is not fully formed and the brain has not reached its fully mature form; however, contamination can occur at any age.

A common example of contamination is *subliminal seduction.*** This was first described by Lloyd Silverman, who spliced pictures of food items into a film so quickly, viewers would not be able to consciously detect them. He found that when he showed pictures of soda, viewers experienced thirst even though they did not "see" the picture of the

*** Silverman, L. S., and C. J. Geisler. 1986. "The Subliminal Psychodynamic Activation Method: Comprehensive Listing Update, Individual Differences, and Other Considerations." Advances in Psychology 38: 49–74.

soda. They believed the feeling of thirst was a signal from their body. The viewers did not even suspect that the feeling of thirst was planted in them.

The four myths discussed in chapter 1 are examples of contamination ideas that parents with symptoms of BPD often insert into the minds of their children. For example, the myth "It is okay to let others hurt you" is contrary to the survival instinct. Children who are raised by parents with symptoms of BPD are often hurt when they are the subject of the parent's lashing out. When they express the hurt, they are often told they deserve it or are ridiculed for being too sensitive. If they attempt to defend themselves, the parent often becomes more aggressive. Eventually, they learn to try to avoid setting the parent off, generally by avoiding the parent. When they are subject to the lashing out, they learn to endure it. They ignore it. After many experiences like this, having others hurt them becomes normalized. At some point, they don't even notice it anymore. When the parent is done lashing out, they expect you to be nice to them as though nothing unusual happened. If you don't resume pleasing them, they claim that you are hurting them. The result is that the child now has a belief that it is alright to let others hurt them.

Verbal lashing out is a common method of contamination. Pejorative statements such as "I wish you were never born," describing a child as "ungrateful" and a "horrible son/daughter," and telling the child, "You ruined my life" contaminate the developing sense of self with a negative self-image.

These statements made repeatedly by your parent have a powerful effect on your view of yourself. You may experience a persistent sense of shame and guilt without being able to understand what you feel guilty about. This is probably because your sense of self was distorted, or contaminated by inaccurate feedback from your parent. This created a sense of your self as bad, wrong, unattractive, etc., without attaching these feelings to specific acts or attributes. Following is the account of ACOB2, who grew up with a mother with symptoms of BPD.

ACOB2: Actual Child of a Parent with BPD Symptoms

From a very young age, I saw myself as unattractive to others and unworthy of their attention and kindness. I felt like I was a burden on others. When I wanted or needed something, I had to either beg or perform—please her in some way. And if I did get what I asked for, there would be a price to pay afterward.

I asked for a ride to college as I entered as a freshman. My college was sixty miles away from my mother's home. I was given a list of chores and errands that I had to do so she could "get ready." I drove in the rain. She complained about the rain and how long it took to load my belongings into the dorm. When she got home, she told me that the drive was "dreadful" and that she felt "awful." The next day, she complained that her back hurt. She brought this up dozens of times over the following years as a way to make me feel guilty or ashamed for not pleasing her in some way or another. It wasn't until thirty years later when I drove my son to college that I realized this task was an honor, not a burden.

I became quiet around others and hid from others when possible. I developed impostor syndrome: I couldn't believe it when someone was kind to me or expressed interest or affection. I felt like I would eventually be found out to be ungrateful or toxic and then rejected.

Projecting and Gaslighting

Parents with BPD use different methods. In addition to contamination, two of the most common, and also most damaging, methods are projection and gaslighting. When children are exposed to these processes throughout their childhood, damage to the self is likely.

Projection

This occurs when your parent projects their thoughts and feelings onto you and then holds you responsible for those feelings. When these thoughts and feelings are repeatedly projected onto the developing sense of self, you tend to take on these thoughts and feelings as though they are your own. Greta was affected so powerfully by the projections of her mother, it almost cost her, her life.

Greta's Story

Greta's mother, Sandy, suffered from symptoms of BPD. She was very concerned about her own appearance and was consistently dieting and trying different clothing, skin treatments, and makeup to optimize her appearance. She thought she was helping Greta by grooming her from a very young age to be thin and to work on her physical appearance. She offered many suggestions and helped her with her hair, makeup, and wardrobe.

Greta hated her body from as early as she could remember. She was repulsed by her physical appearance and felt ugly and unattractive. She tried extreme dieting and exercise, different hair colors, and different clothing, but she never saw herself as attractive. When she got older, she got plastic surgery on her face and other body parts, but she never felt proud of her appearance. She hated looking in the mirror and hated others looking at her.

It didn't help that her mother looked her up and down whenever they got together. Her mother was constantly pointing out how Greta could lose a few pounds or have her hair cut differently. Her friends were baffled by Greta's self-loathing. They told her that she was a beautiful girl, but she didn't believe them. She couldn't see herself that way. The feelings of being unattractive were too deeply rooted.

Greta eventually met a man who fell deeply in love with her. She adored him but felt ashamed about her appearance. She was apologetic to him and tried even harder to improve her appearance. He told her he wanted her to stop trying to change her appearance—he found her very attractive and could not imagine her becoming more attractive to him than she already was. Greta didn't believe him and continued her quest to change her appearance. Her boyfriend couldn't take it anymore and told her that she had to get some psychological help. It hurt him to see her disparage herself.

Greta did visit with a psychologist. She explained to Greta that she had developed body dysmorphic disorder. This caused her to see herself as unattractive no matter what she did to change her appearance. Greta came to realize that she never had a chance to develop a positive view of herself because her mother was constantly finding flaws with her appearance. Her mother had projected her own struggles with her physical appearance onto Greta and they became part of Greta. Once Greta realized she was seeing herself through her mother's eyes, she was eventually able to form her own opinions. Finally, as an adult, she was able to see herself through her own eyes. She learned to accept her appearance and love herself only after she purged herself of her mother's projections.

Gaslighting

Gaslighting occurs when your parent tries to make you believe something that is not true. You are made to feel like there is something wrong with you if you do not believe. This is most damaging to your developing sense of self when the false belief is that you are toxic. Symptoms of BPD often cause parents to avoid taking responsibility for errors or unwanted outcomes by blaming others. When a pattern develops where your parent routinely blames you for unwanted outcomes, it can cause you to develop a sense that you are toxic.

Parents with symptoms of BPD often make comments to their children like "You ruined my life" or "I wish you were never born" when they are frustrated or angry. One parent told his child, "If it weren't for you, I would still be married to your mother." Another parent told her child, "You ruined my career." Another parent blamed the child for his physical illness.

If you were treated this way throughout your childhood, you may have developed a contaminated sense of self. You may see yourself as a pariah. You may have come to believe you are toxic to others. This can cause a persistent sense of guilt, shame, and inferiority.

The Broken Mirror

Children learn who they are in part from the feedback they get from others. This is called "mirroring." Feedback from parents is potent in shaping the child's sense of self. Projection and gaslighting are examples of distorted feedback. Parents with symptoms of BPD often give feedback to their children based on their own feelings or moods or create false perceptions (such as with gaslighting). The parent with BPD is a broken mirror. If your parent offers a broken mirror, you might have developed a distorted, contaminated, or possibly very negative sense of self. The destructive effects of the broken mirror can be so destructive to the developing self that the self is completely neutralized or annihilated.

Annihilation of the Self

The instability of identity, or sense of self, most individuals with symptoms of BPD experience causes them to view themselves and others in black and white, or binary terms. This leads to idealization and devaluation of others, depending on whether or not others please them. When you displease them, they devalue you.

A very common method of this is character assassination. The parent finds every aspect of their child as objectionable and they express this through persistent criticisms of the child's thoughts, statements, ideas, or beliefs. Sometimes, this is stated in general terms, such as, "I wish you were never born" or "You are a loser." At the same time, particular traits may be attacked in statements such as "You are a terrible child," "You are a terrible father," or "You are disgusting—looking at you makes me sick." You might be compared to a culturally condemned figure, such as Hitler, Benedict Arnold, or Archie Bunker.

Devaluating character assassination by a parent always yields distorted feedback. Devaluation is defined as a distortion of perception. Your parent's feedback at these times is based on your parent's emotions (i.e., frustration, anger) and not your behavior. The feedback that you have received to develop a sense of self is not accurate. Exposure to this sort of treatment during the development of your sense of self can have a devastating effect.

As a result of the broken mirror, you learn to define yourself by whether others are pleased by you. You focus on becoming what you perceive others want you to be and avoiding what others do not want. You no longer can tell what your own opinions and preferences are as you do not consider them to be relevant. You may become a completely selfless people pleaser. The self you might have had is annihilated. Jody's experience is a sad example of this.

Jody's Story

As long as she can remember, Jody felt that her father was displeased with her. It seemed like in his eyes, all of her choices were wrong. He thought her television programs were silly and he let her know every time he saw her watching them. He made fun of the shows and mocked them. He used to call her friends the "bad girls" and didn't like them to come and visit. He didn't like the way she liked to wear her hair or the clothes that she wore.

She spent a large portion of her early childhood trying to find ways to please her dad. She didn't wear clothing he didn't like. She asked him to come shopping with her so he could pick out clothes for her. She stopped talking about her friends to him and she never invited them over. She started watching television in her room or while her father was at work. She eventually figured out that the only way her father would approve of her choices was if they were the same as his choices. In his eyes, she brought nothing useful to the table. That's what her mother did. She never argued with her father. She was quiet and obedient.

Once Jody realized this, she understood that her mother wasn't trying to please her father—she was avoiding his lashing out. Jody found herself doing the same thing. Like her mother, she learned to focus on keeping the peace by not making waves but by flying under the radar. She no longer offered ideas or suggestions. She just went along with whatever her father wanted, which was functionally the same as what her mother wanted.

As an adolescent, Jody was the same way with her peers. She had friends. but was known as a follower and not a leader. Her practice of avoiding conflict by not offering ideas or suggestions made her easy to be around, but because she offered nothing, she was of little additional value. She was often overlooked when parties were planned and she was rarely sought after for her opinion or advice. She was never highly respected or in the inner circle of her peer group.

By the time she entered high school, she was so focused on pleasing others, or keeping them from being displeased, she lost the ability to determine her preferences and she no longer sought to develop her ideas; she was made to believe they were worthless. She no longer knew who she was or what she wanted other than to please others and avoid conflict. Like her mother, she experienced annihilation of the self. A state of selflessness. Naturally, she began *to become increasingly depressed. She felt empty, worthless, and without substance, preference, or direction*

Children like Jody who are raised in an environment that is destructive to the formation of the self are at elevated risk for developing reactive mental disorders. Some are able to avoid getting sick by leaving the environment. Some go away to school, join the military, get married, or go live with other relatives. Many children don't have this option. The following are some clinical conditions that can be associated with sustained exposure to a hostile environment during your formative years.

Depression

As Jody experienced, feelings of depression are common in individuals who spend their childhood trying to please a parent who cannot be pleased. The constant criticism attacks your self-confidence and self-esteem. At the same time, you are so outwardly focused, either on pleasing your parent or avoiding your parent lashing out, you completely lose awareness of yourself. These factors often result in feelings of depression and may be associated with a full depressive disorder.

Anxiety

Several different clinical manifestations of anxiety can be associated with being raised by a parent with symptoms of BPD:

- Post-traumatic stress disorder is often found in children exposed to frequent lashing out by their parent. This can include verbal or physical lashing out or both.

- Panic attacks are sometimes associated with fear of the parent lashing out. The parents' unstable behavior always leaves you fearful knowing that you can be targeted at any moment for any reason.

- Generalized anxiety is associated with feeling unsafe with their parents and home and hence unsafe in the world.

- Phobic anxiety can result in avoidance of social situations in general and intimate relationships in particular.

Substance Abuse

The instability associated with being raised by a parent with symptoms of BPD is generally anxiety-producing and uncomfortable to children. The lashing out, gaslighting, and betrayal you experience can produce trauma symptoms. It is natural for individuals in this situation to seek ways to feel less anxious, afraid, and depressed. Many turn to alcohol or other drugs. Use of mood-changing drugs for this purpose often becomes habit-forming.

If you grew up in an environment that is caustic to the development of a healthy sense of self, then you probably struggle with inhibition, contamination, or annihilation of your sense of self. You might also be experiencing clinical symptoms of a mood or anxiety disorder. The next chapter will explain how this affects your current relationships. The remainder of the book will guide you through healing and growth so that you can become the person you were meant to be. The best you can be.

Chapter 4

Impact on Attachment Ability and Relationships

Understanding the effects of growing up with a parent with symptoms of BPD on your current relationships requires an understanding of how this experience has impacted your ability to form emotional attachments to others. In this chapter, you will gain clarity on how your attachment style combined with the modeling of intimate relationships that you were raised with might have compromised your ability to have healthy relationships outside of your nuclear household.

Attachment Types

Emotional attachment between humans is defined by the feelings individuals have toward each other. Being attached to another person means it affects you whether or not they are with you. Different feelings about whether another person is with you or not reflect different types of attachments. The most basic attachment feelings are associated with the attached person's presence or absence.

Positive Attachment

Positive attachment is associated with joy or pleasure when you are with the person and feelings of longing or sadness when they are not present. For example, a relationship has positive attachment when the child protests when the parent drops them off in the morning and then rejoices when the parent picks them up from school. The parent will feel sadness when the child grows up and leaves for college, the military, or a career, but supports the child's growth nonetheless. Growing up in an environment where most attachments are positive results in a positive outlook on relationships in general and the ability to form healthy attachments.

Negative Attachment

When being around someone makes you uncomfortable and being away from them brings you relief, then you are negatively attached to someone. The uncomfortable feelings may include anxiety, fear, anger, shame, or any combination of feelings that cause you to feel less well. In a victim's relationship to a bully, for example, the victim experiences fear and anger when in the vicinity of a bully and relief when they separate. Growing up in an environment where most attachments are negative results in adults who are most comfortable being alone. They don't seek out attachments with others and do not feel comfortable when others try to attach to them.

Mixed Attachment

This type of bond occurs when the object of attachment is unstable. It is the type of attachment that most children of individuals with symptoms of BPD have with their parent. It involves a pattern where the attachment is sometimes positive and pleasant times can be shared, but is sometimes negative for a significant amount of time. If you grew up with a parent who suffers from BPD symptoms, you probably experience anxiety when visiting or thinking of visiting with your parent. The anxiety is caused by an internal conflict between the hope of having a pleasant experience with your parent and the fear of being hurt by your parent based on some past experiences. The inability to know which mood your parent is in and whether the interaction will be positive or negative creates uncertainty and a sense of not being in control, both of which add to the anxiety you experience.

Prolonged exposure to a mixed or an unstable attachment in your formative years can be associated with a generalization of the expectation of instability in all relationships. This often adds to or creates social anxiety.

No Attachment

When two individuals are not attached, they are indifferent as to each other's coming and goings. You are unattached to strangers. There are no feelings other than generic feelings of wanting others to generally experience wellness.

Secure and Insecure Attachments

All attachments can be described as either secure or insecure. The healthiest attachments are secure. These are relationships that have become stable as a result of consistent behaviors and expectations. Secure relationships remain consistent, and hence dependable, regardless of conditions. Each person in a secure attachment treats the other with respect and honor, regardless of their mood at any particular time or whether or not they get their way. These relationships have durable mechanisms of tolerance and compromise. Individuals in secure relationships feel safe to be themselves. They feel accepted and not judged. The safety and security they experience lower stress and anxiety as it provides support and facilitates the wellness of those individuals. The strength and stability of the relationship come from the context, which is a history of many interactions all resulting in positive experiences.

Mixed attachments almost always become insecure. When the person you are attached to is unstable (such as when their behavior toward you is driven more by how they feel rather than how you treat them), the benefit of context is neutralized. The relationship becomes transactional as each meeting redefines the relationship. If you were raised by a parent with symptoms of BPD, you probably experienced periods where you were treated in a friendly or loving fashion and other times when you were treated as the enemy and were targeted with angry lashing out. As a result of this instability and uncertainty, the attachment causes anxiety and is often referred to as an anxious attachment style.

Instead of the safety and support that allows secure attachments to provide comfort, insecure attachments are characterized by frequent, if not constant, testing. This is particularly true when attached to individuals with symptoms of BPD. Fear of abandonment and being alone is a core feature of BPD and causes sufferers to seek constant reassurance that you are present, available, and prepared to respond to them as a priority in your life. The testing generally takes the form of a behavioral challenge that you are not told about until after you fail. Testing can take an infinite number of forms, but here are a few common examples.

The Brutal Clock

This occurs when an individual with symptoms of BPD sets their expectations of when you might contact them without informing you. For example, JP called his mother in response to her leaving him a voicemail. When he called her, they had the following conversation.

JP: Hi, Mom.

Mom: Who is this?

JP: *You only have one son.*

Mom: *Do I?*

JP: *Mom, I am returning your call. What's up?*

Mom: *I thought you forgot my phone number.*

JP: *I just called you.*

Mom: *I called you this morning.*

JP: *Yes, and I am calling you back now.*

Mom: *If you really loved me, you would have picked up the phone or called me right back.*

JP: *I was at the dentist getting a filling.*

Mom: *That takes three hours? I wish you were never born.*

In this example, JP's mother, without knowing what he might be doing at that particular time, lashes out at him for not calling her back fast enough. Only after the lashing out does he become aware that he failed the test of whether he would call her back fast enough.

The Missing Question

This occurs when an individual with symptoms of BPD accuses you of not bringing up some topic and then characterizes the omission as either a character defect or evidence you are not loving or devoted. JP finally got Mom to tell him what she called about, but as the conversation was ending, JP was tested again with the missing question,

JP: *It was nice talking with you, Mom. I love you.*

Mom: *You don't show it.*

JP: *What do you mean?*

Mom:	*Never mind.*
JP:	*I don't understand what is bothering you.*
Mom:	*You are bothering me.*
JP:	*What are you talking about?*
Mom:	*You didn't even bother to ask me about my foot. You don't care about me.*
JP:	*What about your foot?*
Mom:	*Don't you remember I told you I stubbed my toe the other day?*
JP:	*Oh, yes. How is the toe?*
Mom:	*I could drop dead and you wouldn't even notice.*

As you read on, you will realize that these tests are not passable. They are set up so you fail as a way of pushing you away because the parent is in a bad mood. Growing up with your primary attachments being unstable can have a profound impact on how you approach attachment to others as you go through your life.

Effects of Growing Up with an Insecure/ Anxious Attachment to Your Parent

Children of individuals with symptoms of BPD almost always approach others in their lives with the expectation that the attachment will be unstable. Because it was what you experienced throughout your childhood with your parent, unstable attachment now seems normal to you. Unexpected, and often unwelcome, reactions or responses from friends and loved ones are tolerated because you probably have not experienced a stable attachment and thus don't know of anything different. Even if you manage to have a stable relationship with someone else, you probably don't trust it. You have come to expect the aspects of instability described above.

This may also be a self-fulfilling prophecy: your behavior may destabilize your attachments because of how you were raised and what you have come to expect. Understanding how you have normalized destabilizing behavior and may be enabling it will help you to change your expectations about intimacy and attachment and make the changes necessary to enjoy the secure attachments you crave and deserve.

Transactional vs. Contextual Relationships

The instability that individuals with symptoms of BPD experience prevents the formation of secure attachments, resulting in almost all their relationships being transactional. This means that each time you interact with your parent, you have to redefine the relationship by reassuring them that you love them and will not abandon them. If you don't initiate this each time you see them, you will be tested (as previously described).

Conversely, secure relationships are dependent on a context of consistent behavior and reactivity over time, across meetings. A history of consistently healthy and benevolent behavior gives you confidence that each interaction will be positive. Longer relationships with frequent consistent interactions are associated with the highest levels of safety, security, and satisfaction for you and your friend or family member.

People Pleasing

Growing up knowing only transactional relationships probably has trained you to be overly solicitous of others. You anticipate being tested and persistently put the needs of others ahead of your own. You don't express your preferences or your feelings. You just "go with the flow." You focus your attention and your energy on figuring out how to please others rather than getting your own needs and feelings addressed. You believe that anything you do for yourself is selfish and therefore bad.

Selfishness and Selflessness

Most people don't like to be called selfish, but consider its opposite: selfless. "Selfish" refers to looking out for oneself and putting the interests of the self before the interests of others. Parents with symptoms of BPD tend to encourage *selflessness* in their children, using the methods discussed in the last chapter (inhibition of self-development, contamination of the self, and annihilation of the self).

Good and excellent parents, siblings, and friends put the needs of others before their own under extraordinary circumstances, but it is not healthy to always put the needs of others ahead of your needs. As the child of a parent with symptoms of BPD, you were raised to believe selflessness is virtuous and necessary to have someone love and validate you. It was necessary, but often not sufficient, to get your parent to love and validate you. Practicing the selflessness you learned from your parent makes you sick. It diminishes your self-esteem and makes you feel unworthy. This encourages depression. Healthy individuals, however, have a balance of selfishness and selflessness that is adjusted to each situation.

Pleasing people does not get you love, honor, and respect—it gets you used, taken advantage of, and devalued. Love, honor, and respect require that you share yourself with another. How can you do this if you are selfless? You can't. You can only provide service to others. They will appreciate the service, but they don't see *you*. They see a waiter, valet, cook, mechanic, or an ATM. It is the services and goods they are attracted to—not you. Trey found this out the hard way.

Trey's Story

At forty-eight years old, Trey was the same as he was when he was twenty-eight: he just wanted peace in his life. He grew up with a mother with symptoms of BPD and a mild-mannered father who let Trey's mother run the household. Trey and his father did everything they could to please his mother. They were rarely successful in her eyes, but they believed it would be worse if they didn't try. Like his father, he had given up his sense of self in order to be loved, but nonetheless was the subject of frequent criticism and lashing out from his mother much of the time. He felt like his house was in constant conflict; he was anxious and apprehensive most of the time.

He was now looking for a stable relationship, but he had not yet been successful at finding it. Trey was fit, attractive, and a successful corporate lawyer, so he had little difficulty meeting women who he might be attracted to. He dated quite a few of them, but the relationships all seemed to end the same way. He tended to be attracted to strong-willed women, although he didn't understand why. When he met a woman he liked, he did everything he could to please her. His parents had taught him that this is how to get people to like him. He would buy her presents and take her to expensive restaurants and resorts. He cooked for her, cleaned after her, and treated her friends like diplomats.

At first, the women would be flattered and seemed pleased, but then after a few months, they began taking him for granted. Some asked him for money, some favors, others gifts. Many of them became demanding as they became less passionate toward him. They lost respect for him. Some cheated on him. He ended up breaking up with them, feeling exploited. They often got angry at his withdrawal of his attention and indulgence, got angry with him, and accused him of being selfish or damaged.

He realized that while he was seeking a secure and supportive relationship with a woman, he kept finding himself in conflictual insecure pairings. He finally decided to seek professional help. After going over his history with his therapist, he had the following conversation.

Trey: *Doc, what is wrong with me? What am I doing wrong? What am I missing?*

Doc: *Why do you assume you are wrong?*

Trey: *Because I can't get a woman to love me. They love when I serve them.*

Doc: *You think that it is because there is something wrong with you?*

Trey: *What else could it be?*

Doc: *You were raised to believe that if there is a problem in a relationship with a woman, it must be your fault.*

Trey: *How else can I see it?*

Doc: *You try to please women the way you and your father tried to please your mother?*

Trey: *Of course.*

Doc: *Are you looking for a woman like your mother?*

Trey experienced what is often referred to as an "aha moment." He had spent his life up until that point with a gross misunderstanding about how to pursue healthy intimacy with a woman. The joy of epiphany quickly yielded to a disgusted feeling associated with the realization that he was misdirected by his parents and never really even questioned it. This is a feeling that will become familiar to you as you read this book and continue your healing and growth. This feeling is a milestone and should shed light on a different path. You will find joy and satisfaction in following this path. You will recover a part of yourself.

Trust

Trust is the cornerstone of contextual secure relationships. Feelings of trust toward another person occur when the other person is perceived to be consistent and reliable with regard to their behavior toward you and others. This engenders feelings of safety, security, and comfort. Parents with symptoms of BPD tend to parent inconsistently, based on their mood and whether they feel that their child pleases them. If you grew up with an affected parent, you very likely experienced an insecure or anxious attachment. Because you experienced this with your primary attachment during your formative years, you probably have difficulty trusting anyone. The lack of security and stability becomes your expectation as you enter other relationships in your life. Here are some common effects that you may notice in your daily life.

- Perhaps the most pervasive effect of growing up with insecure attachment is that relationships generally make you feel anxious. You are used to routinely being tested, lashed out at, gaslighted, and manipulated, so you enter every interaction with caution and sometimes fear.

- You probably feel safest and most comfortable when you are alone. In extreme situations, you might experience social anxiety and isolation.

- You probably routinely worry others will not show up for meetings or return phone calls or texts in a timely manner.

- You don't expect that others will remember your birthday or other important events in your life.

- You are probably reluctant to ask others for help. You prefer to do things on your own.

- You are reluctant to share your feelings with others.

When you bring these feelings and behaviors into intimate relationships, these feelings inhibit others from trying to securely attach to you. The anxiety you experience is often understood by others as hesitancy, discomfort, or guardedness to those trying to be close to you. Your reluctance to share your feelings, opinions, and preferences is likely to be interpreted as withholding or hiding.

People pleasing can balance these inhibitive factors early in relationships, but they become more difficult to overcome as greater levels of intimacy are sought. This is why Trey was able to engage in short-term relationships, but unable to get satisfaction from intimacy. He would meet women who were attracted to him and held their interest with his people pleasing. As the relationship naturally advanced to deeper levels of intimacy, Trey became increasingly anxious and withdrawn. Women would sense this and feel either rejected or awkward and move on.

Trey approached all women according to this dynamic. He would begin relationships with people pleasing and then hide himself to avoid exposure of his sense of self from attacks, which usually took the form of angry lashing out. Without a complete change of strategy, Trey will never experience the secure attachment that he has always sought.

Trey's behavior is understandable from his experience with his mother. She responded best to people pleasing as her instability prevented her from experiencing deep intimacy. Her strong fear of abandonment focused on Trey being available to her. His feelings, needs, opinions, and preferences were not of interest to her. Rather, she sought to inhibit, contaminate, or annihilate these aspects of Trey that serve to define his sense of self.

If you, like Trey, have spent your life craving intimacy and not finding it, you might be blaming yourself and feeling defective in this area. Or you might have convinced yourself that intimacy in a secure relationship doesn't even exist. If so, you probably suffer some level of loneliness and possibly feelings of depression. If you are willing to take some chances and make some changes, there can be renewed hope. The next chapter will focus on a new strategy and how to convert your current methods to being more effective in intimate relationships.

Triangulation

Individuals with symptoms of BPD often approach security in relationships through control and manipulation rather than empathy, honor, and respect. This frequently takes the form of isolating their children so they can ensure access. A primary mechanism to achieve this is triangulation, where your parent competes with other relatives, friends, and others for your attention and devotion.

The basic format of triangulation is when your parent challenges your devotion or love by demanding that you change your plans to accommodate them. Because your relationship with your parent is likely to be transactional, your history of demonstrating love or devotion in the past is not relevant. You must reinforce this in every single interaction. Does the following conversation sound familiar to you?

Dad: *Can you help me plant some tomatoes this afternoon?*

You: *I would be happy to, but I have some plans this afternoon. How about tomorrow?*

Dad: *What is so important?*

You: *I am hanging out with Jenna.*

Dad: *Didn't you just see her last weekend?*

You: *Yes. But I enjoy being with her.*

Dad: *More than me?*

You: *It is different. You are my dad.*

Dad: *So, I am less important than her?*

You: *It is not about you. I already committed to being with her this afternoon.*

Dad: *How could I have been so stupid to think my son would choose his father?*

Other forms of triangulation that often occur with the basic form is your parent frequently finding fault with your other attachments and making you feel that you have chosen poorly. The most extreme form of triangulation is when the parent forbids you from seeing someone you care about. They justify this by finding some extremely objectionable quality of the person you are fond of. In many cases, this objectionable quality is either a distortion or totally made up. Lia experienced this with her father on the telephone.

Dad: *Lia, where were you?*

Lia: *What do you mean?*

Dad: *I called you earlier and you didn't answer.*

Lia: *I was at a museum.*

Dad: *By yourself?*

Lia: *No.*

Dad: *Who were you with?*

Lia: *Rhona.*

Dad: *That tramp?*

Lia: *She is not a tramp.*

Dad: *All she cares about is being wined and dined on somebody else's dime.*

Lia: *You have no evidence of that.*

Dad: *It is obvious. No daughter of mine is going to be seen with her.*

Lia: *What are you talking about?*

Dad: *Trust me. You should stay away from her.*

Lia: *She is my friend.*

Dad: *It's her or me. Lose her or lose me.*

Growing up in these circumstances has probably left you craving unconflicted closeness with others, but anxious about pursuing it. Your parent has represented to you that liking or loving others hurts them. You see others around you enjoying family groups and friendship groups. You probably have had opportunities to join these groups for periods of time. You might have experienced the closeness of other families during sleepovers or at religious or community-based events. The way you have been raised has programmed you to anticipate conflict and lash out when you participate in these opportunities. You have not developed the skills to be a part of these groups, so you always feel like an outsider. No matter how warm and solicitous others are to you, you still feel anxious and awkward. You are drawn to the idea of being comfortable being close to someone, but it is out of reach. Like Trey, you end up feeling like there is something wrong with you. You may experience trauma symptoms when participating in intimate groups. Avoidance, immobilization, and panic-like states are experienced in the context of a longing for the loving group experiences that others are able to enjoy without conflict.

Creating a Personal Inventory

Personal inventory is never an easy endeavor, but it is an essential process for healing wounds of childhood and unleashing the personal growth that would have occurred naturally had it not been inhibited by the effects of your parent's mental illness. As with physical wounds, psychological wounds must be fully exposed before they can be fully healed. As you pursue a clearer sense of what happened to you and how it affected the development of your sense of self, it can be very helpful to get recollections and perspectives of people who were present during your childhood. This might include relatives, friends, and neighbors. Siblings are particularly helpful. As you listen to the recollections of others, you might be surprised that some of their recollections differ from your own. The instability of your parent's behavior can result in others getting different and possibly even conflicting perspectives.

Nonetheless, even your siblings who grow up in the same household can be treated very differently by your parent, resulting in very different experiences. The tendency for individuals with symptoms of BPD to see things in black-and-white terms and to idealize and devalue those close to them often results in them favoring one child over another. Even this process may be unstable as the transactional nature of their relationships may result in different favorites at different times.

If your parent's symptoms of BPD are severe, you might find aspects of your self-discovery disturbing as long-held beliefs and conceptualizations of your past prove to be myths created and reinforced by your parent's lying and gaslighting. In other words, you may find that you were brainwashed by the person you are supposed to be able to trust above all others. Don't look away. This is your chance to reclaim the lost parts of your self that were inhibited, distorted, and annihilated throughout your childhood by rejecting the distorted mirror and finding the truth.

Understanding how your sense of self was distorted—and reclaiming lost and underdeveloped parts of you—will support your transformation of unhealthy insecure attachments into secure, contextual relationships. You will learn to share yourself with others in a safe and mutually joyful experience rather than trying to get others to love you or prevent them from lashing out at you. The remainder of this book will guide you through the process of healing your emotional wounds and creating the healthy relationships you were meant to have. You will also come to understand the natural process of personal growth and enjoy continued growth throughout your life.

ACOB1: One Man's Experience of Healing and Growth

I supposed therapy, when effective, should transport one from a painful place to a place of understanding, deeper comprehension, and ultimately, strength and peace. My journey in therapy started when I was sixteen years old and still continues over forty years later as I enter my fifty-seventh year. It took me thirty-eight years to understand that I was abused by the person who I trusted most. Recently, I found a few old letters I wrote to my mother. Some are five, ten, or even twenty years old. In each case, I was walking on eggshells in the way I communicated to her.

And this is how she raised me, to walk on eggshells. If she wasn't foretelling stories of my certain future failures in life, if I didn't listen to her grand plan, she was yelling at me as a small boy for slamming a door too loud and waking her on a Saturday morning. At no point was there any concern for the little boy, or how screaming at him with a scary, contorted face might affect him. There was only concern for my mother and, in this particular case, her sacred and undisturbed sleep. It is now fifty years later. I never slam doors, for any reason; I close them gently, even when I'm mad. Somewhere inside me is the traumatized little boy who closed a door too loud one Saturday morning when I was seven. I would never repeat that act.

As I listen to my own small children run around the house in the morning, I hear sounds of laughter and giggling, and sometimes the sound of a door slamming on a Saturday morning while my wife and I are still in bed. Only, in our home, no one gets yelled at for making noise. We delight in those giggles and the high-speed footsteps as they run around being happy children.

I was not so lucky in life; I was not allowed to be a child and I was not allowed to be happy. I was taught from my earliest memories to take care of Mommy. To make Mommy comfortable, to make Mommy happy, to take away Mommy's disappointments regardless of their origin. But I am slowly coming out of my fog. The fog of a life that was all predicated on lies. Lies of all sorts, and lies to cover up lies. One thing was constant: the lack of truth, lack of reality, and lack of normalcy, when you are raised by a borderline mother.

My letters to my mom, which I am reading now, were written when I was in my forties and fifties; but they were written by a scared little boy. Somehow, the letters bear no resemblance to my professional communications during my thirty-five years as a successful CEO. These letters to Mommy all sound the same. "You're great, Mom." "You're right, Mom." "You were always right, Mom." They are squarely deferential. Even when I was standing up to her in my letters, trying to convey strength and ultimatums, they were still written by a boy who was trying to protect Mommy from the truth: she was a terrible mother, a narcissist, and a monster. My tone was firm, yet I was still trying to protect her feelings. I only discovered recently that she has no feelings. She is incapable of any feeling at all.

As I have developed over the last two years of therapy, my understanding of the borderline personality, and my mother, has deepened and grown. Now I see that my mother is powerless to change herself, powerless to feel, and powerless to care about anyone other than herself. She was mentally ill when she was in her mid-thirties, when I was born, and she is still mentally ill at ninety-one. But now, I understand the dynamics that are present in my mother's borderline personality. She is still empty inside. She has not mellowed with age. In fact, she is more virulent now than she was thirty years ago. It's astounding to hear and feel the force with which she speaks. She never softened. She never improved. She never healed. She never did the work to help herself.

But I did. Now, she is powerless over me.

The part of me that was a victim, is no longer. The part of me that was frustrated because I could never get her to hear me, is no longer. The anxiety and tumult that was in my life, is no longer. The feeling of tension that I felt every time she visited and made me or my wife feel bad at the holidays, is no longer. Now, I understand that the borderline personality inside my mother is simply a mental illness. It's not contagious. I can choose to accept the illness or refute the caustic personality that delivers it. I chose to close the door on her. I have the strength to be untouchable.

Today, the scared boy inside me is no longer scared. He doesn't write patronizing notes to his mother. He doesn't run from the conflict of telling her, "No, you're wrong." He doesn't invest time trying to explain things in the hope that she might change her position. She never will. He doesn't attempt to protect her from the world. And he genuinely doesn't allow her mental illness to penetrate his happy family, his happy life, or his successful career. He protects his wife and his small children from suffering the same fate he suffered. Today, he just is, and she isn't. For she was never there at all.

Part 2

Healing

Chapter 5

Creating Strong Interpersonal Boundaries

In part 1, I taught you how to identify wounds of childhood that have persisted into adulthood. A full inventory will probably take you a lifetime, but as you identify each wound, you create the opportunity to heal that wound. Healing is a process, not an event.

Stop the Bleeding

The first step in healing a wound is stopping the bleeding. A cut will not begin to heal with the blade still in it. You cannot heal a burn while lying in the sun. Healing psychological/emotional wounds requires that you first stop the bleeding by creating strong interpersonal boundaries. In simple terms, you must stop others from hurting you if you want to heal.

You might ask me at this point, "How do I know if someone is hurting me?" If you are asking this question, you are very likely the victim of childhood emotional manipulation and abuse. Individuals raised by emotionally healthy parents develop a real-time relationship with pain. They feel pain as it occurs and immediately seek to identify the source. They were raised in an environment where the parents are interested in their pain and discomfort and compassionately partner with the child to bring relief.

In contrast, adult children of parents with symptoms of BPD often freeze up when being hurt by others. This occurs when your childhood experience with identifying and expressing pain to your parent actually increases the pain. If your efforts to seek comfort and relief from pain as a child were consistently thwarted, you probably have come to dissociate. You are strongly inhibited from expressing these feelings because they have historically brought increased pain and discomfort. Rather than feeling the differentiated feelings of pain, discomfort, and anxiety, you just go numb. This is why you routinely freeze up during any conflicts with people you are attached to. You probably think of responses to mistreatment hours or days after it occurs. Perhaps, not at all.

If you experience a level of dissociation that prevents you from experiencing pain when others hurt you, you must learn to defeat the dissociative defense. Without the ability to be aware of others hurting you while they are hurting you, you will not be able to protect yourself and you will not be emotionally well. In the next chapter, I will show you how to defeat your dissociation as we discuss healing from traumatic wounds, but now, we will focus on stopping the bleeding. You must stop others from hurting you before you can heal your wounds.

Defining Boundaries

Before you can set interpersonal boundaries with others, you must define them for yourself. Boundaries should be conceived of based on the function they are intended to fulfill. Some typical functions of boundaries are:

Safety: You have the right to feel safe in relationships and you have the right to not be in relationships that do not feel safe to you. For individuals who have not been raised by parents with personality disorders, this might seem obvious. Having been raised by affected parents, you need to be reminded as often as possible that it is neither healthy nor acceptable to allow others to hurt you. You must reverse the belief that was inculcated in you that you are a bad person for not allowing others to hurt you. This applies to any type of hurt: physical, emotional, financial, or otherwise. If you do not set safety boundaries with others, you almost certainly experience significant anxiety when interacting with others or even thinking about doing so. The "freezing up" described above is the panic-level version of this anxiety.

Wellness: Healthy relationships should add to your general sense of wellness. Healthy, safe, and secure relationships reduce your anxiety due to their supportive nature. They add to your sense of self-value and support confidence and self-esteem. Relationships that are hurtful, disrespectful, or abusive diminish your wellness if you tolerate them. Your healing and growth require that you no longer tolerate them.

Supporting/Facilitating Function: Certain functions in relationships require that specific boundaries be respected. Sexuality is an example, where many people need to feel safe in order to function. Safety often involves having a partner who respects boundaries involving body areas that should and should not be touched during physical intimacy. Other individuals require privacy in order to function.

The need for a boundary usually starts with some sort of discomfort, often anxiety or fear. Individuals behaving in a hurtful or threatening manner create the desire to set a boundary to restore control and/or safety. Successful setting of a boundary is associated with relief from these uncomfortable feelings.

The next step is to define the boundary in behavioral terms. This involves a description of acceptable and unacceptable behaviors. The elements of boundaries usually involve either physical behavior (such as inappropriate touching of one's body or possessions) or emotional behavior (usually defined by verbal behavior or how you are spoken to).

Common examples of setting physical boundaries include requiring roommates or siblings to ask before borrowing clothing or defining acceptable and unacceptable ways others may touch you. Emotional behavioral boundaries can concern many different aspects of how others might talk to you. Examples can include tone, content, or timing. A generalized form of this boundary is explained below.

Using the Form Before Content Boundary Tool

Utilization of this very effective boundary tool requires that you think about verbal communication in two dimensions. The content dimension is what you are talking about; form is the way of talking. Content can include anything from a discussion about what to have for dinner to sharing important or interesting information, such as new events or scheduling. The form of communication involves characteristics such as tone, aggressiveness, or respectfulness.

Use of the form before content tools involves refusing to address content unless the form is at least civil and, ideally, respectful. Naturally, it is very important that you also speak in the tone that you expect of others (generally respectful). Being respectful to others will increase your self-respect. This will be discussed in detail in chapter 9 as part of your growth strategy. In the following dialogue, Joe uses the form before content tool with his father, who has symptoms of BPD.

Dad: *Joe, I need some help refinishing the deck. Get your work gloves.*

Joe: *I was just leaving to meet Cindy.*

Dad: *She can wait.*

Joe: *You want me to stand up my fiancée to help you stain the deck?*

Dad: *You use it, don't you?*

Joe: *I don't mind helping you with the deck, but can't we find a mutually convenient time?*

Dad: *Oh, so I am just a convenience to you?*

Joe: *Dad, I am just asking for a little notice.*

Dad: *Forget it, go be with your nasty little girlfriend. I wish I never had children.*

Joe: *I am willing to work this out with you, but not while you are insulting and hurtful.*

Dad: *I am your father. I will talk to you any way I please.*

Joe: *I will no longer talk to you unless you treat me in a civil fashion.*

Dad: *Just tell Cindy you will see her tomorrow and get your gloves.*

Joe: *I told you that I am not going to speak to you when you use this tone.*

Dad: *Oh, now you are little Mr. Big Man.*

Joe: *This conversation is over. If you would like to discuss this in a civil fashion, we can pick it up later.*

It is imperative at this point that Joe supports his boundary by ending the conversation until his father decides to speak to him with at least a civil tone. If throughout Joe's life he ignored his father's aggressive tone and addressed the content anyway, his father would expect him to continue doing so. As in the above example, he is likely to escalate his aggression in response to Joe's initial effort to set the boundary. For this reason, Joe must make it clear that his father's nasty tones are no longer acceptable. If Joe is able to be consistent with this boundary, eventually, his father will most likely begin to speak to him in a more acceptable tone.

Setting Healthy Boundaries in Intimate Relationships

Healthy individuals have healthy boundaries and don't need you to set boundaries for them. They naturally respect others as it increases their respect for themselves. They strive to see themselves as respectful and feel most confident and worthy when they express this aspect of themselves.

Some individuals are not so healthy with their own boundaries, but they are receptive to the boundaries of others when articulated in a way that is meaningful to them. For example, if you ask them to remove their shoes before entering your carpeted living room, they graciously comply. They do not express that they are burdened or insulted by the request. They are grateful you are working with them to make them comfortable in your home and you are comfortable with them in your home. It sets a healthy context for an enduring and respectful relationship. Individuals who are healthy enough to be receptive to your boundaries rarely have to be told twice. They understand healthy relationships honor the boundaries of others and in doing so honor the relationship. They prioritize remembering boundaries so they can negotiate them without conflict.

In contrast, people who resist or test boundaries tend to have difficulties in relationships. Their resistance is almost always experienced as uncooperative, hurtful, and offensive. The need to set boundaries is initiated by pain or discomfort. The boundary is meant to relieve the discomfort through accommodation in the relationship. The resistance or refusal to cooperate in this area undermines trust and attraction. Parents suffering from symptoms of BPD often see their children's pain or discomfort as an indication of their failure as parents. When you tell them they are hurting you or making you uncomfortable, they see it as an accusation or indictment rather than an opportunity to provide comfort or support by negotiating a healthy boundary. This often leads to a form of lashing out and you get hurt more. The following exchange between Ali and her mother is an example.

Ali: *Mom, can Barky stay with you this weekend?*

Mom: *What am I, a dogsitter?*

Ali: *I am going to be away and I thought maybe you would enjoy having him.*

Mom: *Sure, at least I am good for something.*

Ali: *What are you upset about?*

Mom: *My daughter only contacts me when she needs something.*

Ali: *That is not true. I call you almost every day.*

Mom: *You just go away whenever you want and don't worry about me.*

Ali: *I just thought you might want to spend the weekend with Barky.*

Mom: *Why don't you want to spend the weekend with me? I am only worthy of the dog?*

Ali: *Mom, you are hurting me. Why are you trying to make me seem like a bad daughter?*

Mom: *Because you are. I wish you were never born.*

Ali's mother saw watching the dog as a rejection. She expressed this to Ali in unkind ways. When Ali expressed her feelings and tried to discuss them, her mother lashed out at her more. She blamed Ali for her own pain rather than acknowledging that she might be causing it. Ali got this message from her mother over and over again: if Ali was uncomfortable or suffering in any way, it was her fault and her problem.

Experience of pain or discomfort is supposed to drive you to seek comfort and relief. When you are consistently thwarted in your attempts to find relief, significant anxiety routinely accompanies these already unpleasant feelings. The anxiety is the result of the anticipation of being thwarted in efforts to find relief from discomfort or pain. Even when you express pain to your parent that was not caused by them, you might get a hurtful response. This typically occurs when you share feelings of discomfort or pain with your parent and they attempt to assuage your feelings by telling you how to deal with those who are causing the unpleasant feelings. Conflict occurs when you either don't follow the parent's suggestion, or when you do follow it, but it does not work. Under these circumstances, the parent feels invalidated by you and may lash out at you. This happened to Hank when he confided in his father about a situation at work.

Dad: *How are things at work?*

Hank: *Could be better.*

Dad: *What's going on?*

Hank: *I am worried I might get fired.*

Dad: *Why would they do that?*

Hank: *A few of the customers complained I was not attentive to them.*

Dad: *Don't worry about it. There are always people who are unhappy with service.*

Hank: *I got a stern warning from my supervisor. I am very worried.*

Dad:	*You should tell your supervisor not to listen to unhappy customers.*
Hank:	*Dad, that's not the way it works at this store.*
Dad:	*You stand up and tell them the way things should be run.*
Hank:	*I can't do that.*
Dad:	*Then you deserve to be fired.*

Hank learned from this exchange that his father either was not willing or not capable of being supportive in work-related matters. On the contrary, his father made it about him and then lashed out at Hank for not following his suggestion. Hank would do well to create a healthy boundary with his father where Hank does not discuss his work troubles with his father.

Setting such a boundary does not need to be confrontational. Hank can just omit sharing work-related information with his father and instead steer his conversations with his father to other topics. If his father asks about work, he can simply say, "Nothing new" or "Everything is fine" and most likely his father will drop it. If Hank finds that his father only behaves this way around work-related topics, then Hank's boundary should only apply to the withholding of work-related matters.

If Hank's father was emotionally healthy, Hank might attempt a confrontational approach in an attempt to salvage some intimacy with his father. He might say, "Dad, I want to share my feelings with you, but I can't do so if you respond to me in a hurtful manner." However, if Hank's father has significant symptoms of BPD, this will probably not work. As part of the pattern of blame shifting that is common in BPD sufferers, Hank's father is likely to respond with something like "You need to grow a thicker skin." When you express hurt feelings to someone and they tell you to grow a thicker skin, they are essentially telling you that you should get better at letting people hurt you. This message is the opposite of a loving response. Parents who love their children are naturally compelled to protect their children from harm and do not encourage their children to allow themselves to be hurt more.

If Hank's father is apologetic, which is not common in situations where BPD symptoms are involved, Hank might continue to share his feelings with his father. He can continue to do so as long as his father is successful at not lashing out at him. Again, this is not typical because the lack of empathy and impulsivity in the expression of anger prevent this type of healthy behavior. In this case, Hank will have to cease his efforts to share emotions with his father.

If Hank finds that his father is unsupportive and in many situations undermines Hank's confidence when he tries to share difficult situations with him, then Hank will need to create a more general boundary. An example of a more general boundary might involve not sharing any uncomfortable feelings with his father or not sharing feelings at all. Hank had to set a general boundary of not sharing any feelings with his father when he tried to share feelings of joy with his father and was still verbally attacked.

> Hank: *Dad, I had a great time fishing yesterday. I caught a 25-lb. bass.*
>
> Dad: *I am so glad you had time to go fishing yesterday while your mother and I cleaned the house.*
>
> Hank: *You didn't ask me to help you clean the house.*
>
> Dad: *Did I ask you to mess it up?*

If your efforts to share your feelings with others consistently garner a hurtful response, you must stop sharing your feelings with that person. When you set boundaries with someone with symptoms of BPD, they might accuse you of punishing them, by withholding. This is not punitive—it is protective. You should not feel guilty for protecting yourself or your loved ones. You cannot experience a healthy level of self-esteem or self-worth if you don't protect yourself. Anything of value deserves to be protected.

When people you are trying to be close to either refuse to honor your boundaries, resist them, or mock them, it puts a major limitation on the intimacy you can experience with them. Intimacy requires trust based on safety and security. When someone you are trying to be close to is not cooperative with your boundaries, you must make a choice. You can try to be intimate with such a person anyway. In doing so, you accept that the person will not consistently make efforts to increase your comfort and you will suffer in the relationship.

On the one hand, some boundary violations are just annoying. A person who interrupts you frequently is an example. Another example is someone who borrows your belongings without asking or returns them dirty or damaged. You may choose to tolerate relationships such as this, but you are unlikely to enjoy them. You will prefer to be around other people who eagerly accept or honor your boundaries. On the other hand, other physical and/or psychological boundary violations are truly harmful to you. In chapters 2 and 3, you learned that these violations can be traumatic and cause extensive damage to your sense of self, especially the developing sense of self. Sustaining relationships such as these without substantial modification is a direct assault on your health and therefore not recommended. Interactions with individuals who violate and do not cooperate with your boundaries necessitate constant vigilance and guarded preparedness on your part. Your need to protect yourself in this way will almost certainly eliminate any aspect of intimacy that might develop with such a person.

Incompatible Boundaries

Those who persist in disrespecting your boundaries leave only one other option: to end the relationship altogether. In this circumstance, you are being confronted with an unhealthy proposition: You must endure discomfort, hurt, or abuse to be in a relationship with them. You are forced to accept a form of masochism to be in their world.

This is their choice to set such a boundary and you need not feel guilty for declining such an offer. Even if it is with a parent.

Setting Healthy Boundaries in Non-intimate Relationships

To experience the full benefits of healthy boundaries in your life, you must be prepared to set them in all relationships, not just with your parent, life partner, or child. If you set boundaries with your parent, but allow others to mistreat you, you fragment your sense of self. You create a circumstance where it is alright for some people to mistreat you in certain circumstances. You behave in a self-protective way in some situations, but allow others to hurt you in others. Emotional health requires stability, which requires consistent expression and treatment of the self. The techniques of setting boundaries are the same in intimate and non-intimate relationships, but it is essential that you consistently set and reinforce such boundaries to be well. This will be discussed in detail in chapters 8 and 9 as part of your pathway toward growth. But first, you must stop the bleeding and then heal.

Strong Boundaries Make Secure Relationships

Healthy intimate relationships can only be enjoyed by individuals with healthy personal boundaries and a willingness to honor and respect the boundaries of others. Successful navigation of healthy intimate relationships requires a consistent awareness, or mindfulness, of your own boundaries and the boundaries of others. There must be a consistent willingness to champion the well-being of the other at all times. Even when in conflict, or when you don't get your way.

This attitude toward others who you are intimate with not only facilitates solving conflicts but also converts each conflict into an opportunity to strengthen the relationship and enhance the intimate component of the relationship. Showing caring and respect while resolving differences in opinion or preference emphasizes the integrity of the relationship over being right or getting your way. The benefits to the relationship of being maintained this way convert a competitive (win-lose) situation into a cooperative (win-win) one. This is a bonding experience that makes relationships more stable and more durable.

Transactional vs. Contextual Relationships

Relationships with insufficient or no boundaries are transactional. The lack of agreement about what is acceptable and non-acceptable behaviors causes destabilization of the relationship. Each interaction requires renegotiating the definition of acceptable. With individuals who suffer symptoms of BPD, such as emotional dysregulation, the definitions may depend on the person's mood on any given day. They might tolerate some behaviors when they are in a good mood and then lash out when they are dysregulated. Individuals with symptoms of BPD can become dysregulated at any time and very quickly resulting in lashing out behavior toward you. This type of functioning can only produce a transactional relationship.

Transactional relationships are uncomfortable due to their instability and unpredictability. The dysregulation creates a sense that you never know what you will find when you interact with an emotionally unstable person. This produces anxiety and fear. Behaviors that do not reflect concern for your well-being can result in acts of humiliation that will produce shame and anger. Transactional relationships are unstable and uncomfortable and therefore cannot be intimate to any significant degree.

Contextual relationships, in contrast, are defined by patterns of behavior over time and across events. Individuals who have healthy boundaries treat each other in consistent ways, resulting in predictability, safety, and security. These relationships are not redefined depending on one person's mood. The predictability associated with such consistency results in the minimization of fear and anxiety as trust and intimacy grows.

ACOB2

I didn't realize it, but throughout my childhood, I was afraid of people. I grew up in a household with a parent who hurt me on a regular basis. When my mother was displeased, she would make me feel more displeased. Sometimes, it was in the course of a disagreement, but other times, it was out of the blue. Without provocation, she would tell me she wished I was never born or that I ruined her life. Even as an adult, she would periodically bring up that I caused her to have pain during delivery.

I was never allowed to protest. If I told her not to say things like that to me, she got angrier and explained that after what I put her through by being such a bad child, I deserved to be treated this way. If I resisted, she cursed me and told me that I was a horrible son and a repulsive person.

I still had the desire to be around others. I preferred peers because adults were too scary. I was brought up to believe that adults could hurt me at their whim and there was nothing I could do to stop them. Dealing with adult women, like my friends' mothers or schoolteachers, especially terrified me. I often found myself unable to talk or think in front of them.

It took me thirty years and a failed marriage to finally meet someone who let me know that she was interested and concerned about my comfort and wellness. Her behaviors consistently followed her words. I realized then that I had never been loved before, even though I thought I had. My life turned a corner at this time that was a point of no return. I didn't have to be afraid of people anymore because I was allowed to protect myself. People who love me want me to protect myself.

Consistently setting and reinforcing healthy boundaries in all your relationships will stop the bleeding. It will stop the damage to your confidence, self-esteem, and sense of self-worth. It will provide a sense of control that will give you an experience of safety and diminishment of anxiety and fear. You are allowed to protect yourself and encouraged to do so.

Now you are ready to begin the healing process. In the next two chapters, I will guide you through healing traumatic and non-traumatic wounds and injuries, which will restore your process of personal growth. You will no longer be stuck in hurtful relationships. You will finally be free. And soon, you will know deep in your heart that you will never go back.

Chapter 6

Healing Trauma Wounds

Now that you have stopped the bleeding, it is time to begin to heal your wounds. If your boot causes a blister on your foot, you must remove the boot before the wound can heal. If you put the boot back on during the healing process, the wound will quickly return. If keep the boot on at this point, the wound will just get deeper and more painful until you stop the bleeding permanently. Similarly, your attempts to bring yourself relief from your relationship wounds will be neutralized if you continue to allow others to hurt you. First, you must be able to distinguish between traumatic injury and serious injury.

Traumatic Injury vs. Serious Injury

Young children are particularly vulnerable to traumatic injuries because their lack of life experience and not yet fully developed brains increase the chances a dangerous or threatening event will cause traumatic injury. Separation from a parent is a minor, but painful injury and can cause a young child tremendous distress. Their ability to cope is completely overwhelmed and they experience panic-like symptoms. They typically need to be consoled by a trusted person to recover.

Comprehensive preparation, particularly for adults, can prevent traumatic reactions to events that most adults would find traumatic. Police, military, and first responders are prepared to deal with death and violence as part of their training. This helps prevent traumatization when these events occur. The difference between a traumatic injury and a non-traumatic serious injury is not simply a function of the intensity of the assault or the pain it leaves behind but instead depends on each individual's *preparedness* for the event. Traumatic wounds occur when the nature of the event is beyond the realm of what the person would consider possible.

Traumatic injuries have different psychological symptoms than serious injuries. A very common symptom is shock. This experience involves a temporary interruption in the ability to process information. People are literally unable to think or act immediately following a traumatic experience. Individuals in shock may be unresponsive, even though they are conscious and awake.

Non-traumatic serious injuries can be extremely damaging, even life-threatening, but they will not cause traumatic wounds if there is an adequate level of previous consideration and preparedness. For example, surgeries often involve having your body cut open and altered in some way while you lie there helpless. Good surgeons and their team prepare people for surgery by telling them in advance what to expect. This mitigates an emotionally traumatic reaction to the surgery in most circumstances. (It should be noted that there may be trauma associated with finding out that you have an illness that you never thought would be possible. This aspect of trauma will not be mitigated by preparation for surgery. This aspect has to be addressed separately.)

Regression

The shock of exposure to trauma during childhood often stops development. Without healing, when faced with similar situations, you may react to these situations in ways that are childlike as an adult. Your perceptions and understanding of what you see and hear may be interpreted in a childlike manner, resulting in a regressive experience. This happened to Lynn almost every time she was involved with her mother.

Lynn's Story

Lynn is a thirty-seven-year-old bank vice president. She is well-respected and expected to be promoted in the near future. She regularly runs meetings with the managers who work for her and is known to be sober and mature, even by managers who are older than her. She is confident and competent at work.

Her entire demeanor changes when she interacts with her mother. The following dialogue is an example.

Mom: *Lynn, I need to get a new winter jacket. Will you take me to the mall this Saturday?*

Lynn: *I am sorry, Mom, I already have plans.*

Mom: *Oh. What is so important?*

Lynn immediately became flustered and confused. She felt tongue-tied. At that moment, her mind went blank and she became very anxious. In a quiet, childlike tone, she replied.

Lynn: *I am going to be with my friend.*

Mom: *Which friend?*

Lynn knew from past experience that when her mother asked her to justify not doing what her mother wanted that her mother would pick apart her explanation and lash out if she did not get her way. She knew that she was walking into a trap, but she could not think of anything to do but keep answering her mother's questions.

Lynn:	Gene.
Mom:	*What a loser.*
Lynn:	*He is not a loser.*
Mom:	*If you choose being with Gene over me, then you are a loser,*
Lynn:	*I will take you to the mall on Sunday.*
Mom:	*Never mind. Go with your paramour. I will get my own coat. You are useless anyway.*
Lynn:	*Okay. I will see if Gene can meet on Sunday so I can take you on Saturday.*

Lynn thought, What just happened? *She felt disoriented and queasy. She agreed to change her plans because her mother bullied her. She barely remembered the conversation. She felt like she had no choice but to give in to her mother. She was at that moment very far from the bank vice president position when not around her mother. She was so sick, she was unable to eat for the rest of the day.*

The next day, she started to feel better, but still decided it was easier to change the meeting with Gene than face her mother's wrath. Gene was willing to be flexible. Unfortunately, the next time she had a conflict with her mother, Lynn experienced the same traumatic symptoms again. She lost herself and became a helpless little girl.

Lynn's regression was facilitated by her mother treating her like a child and not like the successful businessperson that she is. Asking Lynn to justify not taking her on Saturday and then attacking her answer is disrespectful. It conveys that she views Lynn as too immature to make proper judgments, so Lynn's mother takes it upon herself to correct Lynn's judgment. Lynn's mother lashes out at her if she still does not acquiesce and retraumatizes her. Lynn needs to stop the bleeding ASAP.

Dissociation

Dissociation to some extent is almost always present in trauma victims. This symptom involves the sense of not being fully present, almost like being in a daydream. This was why Lynn had difficulty recalling parts of the conversation. She was not fully present.

The term "dissociation" refers to a broad spectrum of experiences. The mildest form is daydreaming. Most people experience periods of time when they are so focused on their own thoughts, feelings, and fantasies to the extent that the current environment recedes into the background of their awareness. While daydreaming, you might miss details of conversations or other aspects of your surroundings, but you maintain some awareness of your surroundings.

Intense forms of dissociation can be associated with a complete loss of awareness of the current environment. This is often debilitating. It can be associated with all sorts of hazards such as getting on the wrong train at a station, not seeing a vehicle approaching dangerously, or failing to identify other harmful aspects of the environment. Auto accidents occur when individuals dissociate while driving and veer from the lane or road altogether.

Severe dissociation may result in fugue states, when traumatized individuals do not remember the traumatic event at all. Individuals find themselves in environments or situations and have no recollection of how they got there. This is akin to the blackouts experienced by excessive alcohol use, but occurs without ingesting substances. Sexual acts and criminal acts sometimes occur during these periods without any recollection of those events. In extreme situations, this can result in amnesia for events that occurred over hours or even days. In trauma survivors, regression occurs during dissociated periods and is the cause of "repressed memories" of childhood trauma.

Dissociation is a defense against trauma. It is a method of removing the self from a hazardous situation when it is not possible to remove the body from assault. Without healing, trauma victims are generally not in control of the onset of dissociation. They experience it as automatic whenever they are in a situation similar to a past trauma. They generally don't realize they have been absent until they return.

The most extreme form of dissociation is the development of multiple personality disorder (MPD). MPD is rare but does occur. It happens when a child is exposed to persistent and extreme trauma throughout their childhood. The shock of the trauma fragments the developing self to such an extent that the different fragments develop separately into different personalities. Some of those personalities appear to protect the other personalities from the attacks on the self. Lynn does not have this level of dissociation. MPD generally occurs when there is both physical and emotional trauma constantly throughout childhood.

Healing trauma wounds requires that the processes of regression and dissociation be addressed. As described above, these processes interact with and perpetuate each other, resulting in you getting stuck. You handle relevant situations in the same way each time even though they produce unsatisfactory results.

Lynn and her mother above illustrate this process. When Lynn's mother challenges her judgment during conflicts, Lynn gets anxious: this scenario is familiar to her and painful every time. Lynn's initial reaction is dissociation, which was associated with her sense of being stunned or shocked. This indicates that previous similar experiences were traumatic to her to some extent. The disruption of her ability to think clearly compromises her ability to respond to her mother in an optimal way, so she regresses to a childlike state. This retraumatizes her and makes future similar events, especially with her mother, more likely to cause her to experience dissociation and regression. She must break this chain.

Mindfulness Neutralizes Dissociation

As a survivor of persistent childhood emotional trauma, you probably developed a pattern of dissociation that is so pervasive and persistent you don't even recognize it as an altered state. You learned to go through your childhood with minimal awareness, yet the dependency for survival on your parent prevents you from physically removing yourself. So, you learned to remove awareness, or dissociate, as a coping mechanism. Now that you are no longer in such an environment (since you stopped the bleeding), you have to find a way to be present for your adulthood.

The only way to neutralize dissociation is with increased mindfulness. Mindfulness is the opposite of dissociation. Increasing mindfulness is the result of increased awareness of the here and now. Mindfulness requires that you focus your attention on your surroundings and your reactions to your environment in the form of thoughts and feelings.

There are many approaches to increasing mindfulness including meditation, dialectical behavior therapy, and spirituality. These approaches are all effective as they involve training yourself to actively focus your attention rather than passively reacting to perceived threats followed by avoidance. There are many exercises offered by the various approaches and they will all benefit you if you practice them regularly, but to benefit optimally from these techniques, you must stop being afraid of your environment. This is why you must stop the bleeding.

Remember: The primary mechanism for stopping the bleeding is setting and reinforcing interpersonal boundaries. Your confidence in your ability to do so will decrease your fear of your environment and provide a sense of safety, stability, and comfort, which will facilitate your effectiveness and reward your efforts to be more present. Growing up in a persistently unstable and dangerous environment took away your ability to tolerate being yourself. There was too much pain and fear associated with the frequent lashing out, character assassination, and gaslighting. Now that the bleeding has stopped, you can exercise the ability to create a safe and stable environment for yourself. Being present—mindfulness—is at the cornerstone of this process.

ACOB2

I spent my childhood wishing it was over. I didn't understand then, but I understand now that I was constantly intimidated and terrorized. I got relief whenever I could get away. Going to school, a friend's house, or visiting with my grandparents was my only relief. Returning home was like plunging into darkness. I yearned for sleep to bring the next day so that I could get at least a few hours of relief.

It got so bad in high school, each day, I would come home and my back and neck would go into spasm as I anticipated the lashing out and manipulation. The spasms were so painful, I was in tears until I was able to get into bed and go to sleep.

My mother could neither conceive of nor tolerate the possibility that she might be contributing to or causing my symptoms, so she sent me to a psychiatrist. Pure gaslight. I visited with the doctor two times and told him of my symptoms and my plight. At the end of the second session, he told me the problem was my mother and I was doing the best anyone could do under the circumstances. He suggested I minimize contact with her until I finished high school and then go away to college.

There might have been some relief that the doctor did not think I was mentally ill. He also validated that I was being raised by a very toxic parent. Unfortunately, he offered me no hope but to get out as soon as I could. My childhood was over, if it ever really existed. I followed his advice. This provided some relief, but it still took many years before I would understand how much of myself I had lost and begin my journey to reclaim.

This will probably be very scary and disorienting at first. You were punished for being you. Lashed out at for your opinions, thoughts, and preferences if they differed from your parent's. You dissociated from yourself because it was not safe to be you. At the same time, you were forbidden to leave. Any inclination to venture away from home or to befriend anyone other than your parent is always discouraged and often punished. You couldn't stay in the present and you couldn't make a future, so you had to disappear. The practice of mindfulness will turn your light back on. It does this by increasing your awareness of your surroundings while at the same time increasing your self-awareness.

Your healing starts now. It will be scary at first, but with time, you will experience a level of comfort and stability you never dreamed was attainable. Stop the dissociation and be present. Learn to be comfortable with yourself. Treat yourself with honor, respect, and compassion. Learn to insist that others around you also treat you this way. Let the sunshine in, finally.

Intrapsychic Boundary

When you have increased your mindfulness to the extent that dissociation is minimized, you will be able to use more mature and effective coping mechanisms to support your mental health. A very important method is the development of an intrapsychic boundary. An intrapsychic boundary is a type of filter that allows you to scrutinize the words and actions of others and then focus on messages that you consider valid and helpful and dismiss invalid and hostile communications.

As a child, if you were told by your parent that you were selfish and ungrateful, you were treated as though this were true and punished for it. Efforts to convince your parent that they were incorrect were always unsuccessful and often resulted in more anger, lashing out, and punishment. This gave you another reason to dissociate and you probably abandoned your own perspectives and opinions as they had no function since they could not be expressed.

Instead, when this happens, reflect on your experiences with this person and decide whether their statement is valid or not. If valid, you will adjust your behavior and feel good about having done so. If you decide their opinion is not valid, you will use the intrapsychic boundary to dismiss these accusations and feel good about that. You will no longer surrender your perspectives and sense of well-being just because other people give you distorted feedback or attempt to gaslight you. This will markedly increase stability and security in all your relationships; greater confidence and control make you more interpersonally effective.

Take on Regression

Episodes of regression involve you feeling, thinking, and acting like a child. When these experiences occur during interpersonal conflict, particularly those involving a person who has the propensity and inclination to be hurtful or abusive, these experiences can be debilitative. Your ability to think, feel, and behave like an adult is necessary to protect yourself and keep yourself safe.

Another step in neutralizing regression is becoming aware that you are in a regressive state. Mindfulness will be your primary tool. General practice of mindfulness involves training yourself to regularly and habitually check in with yourself throughout the day. Some of the people who I work with set their computers or other electronic devices to beep every half hour as a reminder. When they hear the tone, they stop what they are doing and focus their attention on themselves. They check in on how they are feeling and how they are functioning.

Many people who I work with are capable of such intense focus on their work that they completely lose access to self-awareness. This often results in dehydration, low blood sugar, and even not going to the bathroom in a timely fashion. Most of these people are highly successful in their professions, but they also suffer from illnesses that can be associ-ated with neglecting their feelings and needs. Examples of such illnesses are kidney stones from dehydration, bladder disorders from excessively holding urine, and constipation from retaining feces. Immediately begin this practice of regularly checking in with yourself throughout the day, if you are not already doing so. Over time, this will become natural and habitual and will require less and less effort.

As the child of a parent who suffers from BPD, you were probably discouraged from mindfulness. You were expected to focus on your parent and accused of being selfish for focusing on your own needs. You were expected to eat when it was convenient for them to feed you, not when you were hungry. One man grew up in a small apartment with only one bathroom. As a child, he was not allowed to use the toilet in the morning as his mother reserved it for her use. This man developed significant lifelong bowel issues as a result.

To survive an emotionally abusive childhood, you had to learn to respond to danger by shutting down your awareness (dissociation) and letting the child in you take over. Indeed, going from full awareness to dissociation is a distinctive feeling. This shift—from mindful awareness to dissociated regression—you must become sensitized to. In childhood, you were trained to ignore this feeling (along with all other feelings). Now, you must turn this into an alarm. Once you are able to do this, this sensation will join natural alarm systems (such as smelling smoke, hearing loud noises, or people screaming) that do not need constant monitoring. Rather, they impose themselves into your awareness so that you cannot help but stop what you are doing and address them with urgency.

I understand that this initially sounds overwhelming. The idea that your ability to know how you feel, who you are, and most importantly how to protect yourself was taken away from you as a child is profound. Your parent's impact on your development has frozen aspects of your development early in your childhood by a parent who wanted you to be who they wanted you to be and not your natural self. You will remember this moment as the beginning of the process of taking back your self and your faculties. You will finally become who you were meant to be, who you want to be. This will take time. Be patient. In the remainder of this book, I will guide you through this process. There will be frustration and there will be pain, but if you stay with the mechanisms of healing and growth, you will emerge with a sense of wellness that you never dreamed possible. It will be worth every drop of your blood, sweat, and tears.

Once you are aware of being in a regressed state, you must immediately exit from that state. Like waking up from general anesthesia after a medical procedure, you must first look around and orient yourself to your surroundings. You must then check in with yourself and assess your state. Most urgently, you must assess your ability to function as an adult in the current circumstance.

In the above example, Lynn was only able to regain adult awareness after she had compromised herself with her mother, not during the conversation. As soon as her mother challenged her, she felt a familiar but foreboding feeling. She had been trained to dissociate and regress by her mother's persistent lashing out, so she became disarmed and succumbed. You will learn to recognize this feeling and then assess your state. If you are able to, you will defeat the regression and respond in an adult and mature fashion. With Lynn, defeating the regression would entail setting a boundary with her mother she will not negotiate: her right to say no. This might sound something like this:

Lynn: *Mom, I told you I can't go with you this afternoon. Asking me to justify this to you is disrespectful to me.*

If you are not able to maturely respond in the moment, you can say, "I will get back to you" and respond when you can or when you choose. If you are in a position where you are physically compromised, you need to do whatever you must to remove yourself from that situation and then assess your state in an atmosphere of physical safety.

You have now learned how to identify and neutralize dissociation and regression when you experience it. Having a stable and peaceful life requires that you eliminate trauma from your life as much as possible. This will require you to deprogram the childhood gaslighting. You were programmed to believe that mistreatment and abuse are normal in close relationships and that you must tolerate such treatment if you are in one. You were also trained to believe that any effort on your part to stop others from hurting you, or to even acknowledge that they are, is offensive and you are selfish and ungrateful for doing so.

Remember: These beliefs are neither normal nor healthy. You need to stop tolerating hurtful or disrespectful treatment on the first occurrence. You do not wait for circumstances to become traumatic before you act. This applies to *all* relationships, not just with your parent. Trevor learned this the hard way.

Trevor's Story

Trevor was raised by a mother who suffered from severe symptoms of BPD. As far back as his memory goes, he could recall instances when his mother lashed out at others, usually when she did not get her way, but sometimes just for entertainment. Everyone tolerated it and most ignored it. Mostly, she lashed out at his dad. When his dad left, she would lash out at boyfriends. Eventually, they left too. Trevor often saw her lash out at her father, who would sometimes protest but ultimately gave in to her every time without consequence. Trevor argued with her, debated her, placated her, and even begged her. These methods often resulted in more lashing out. He asked his grandfather for help. His grandfather told him she had issues and nothing could be done. His grandfather urged him to be tolerant and understanding. He followed his grandfather's guidance until he finished high school. He developed significant symptoms of anxiety, but he avoided her as much as possible, tolerated his symptoms, and then left right after graduation.

Though Trevor was relieved to get away from his abusive
mother, he was starved for affection and companionship.
He sought affection wherever he could find it. Early into
relationships with women, mistreatment occurred on several
occasions, but Trevor barely noticed. When he did, he thought his
girlfriend was being spunky or extroverted. For example, she would
say unkind things about him in front of his friends. When she
promised to pick him up at work but did not show up because her
friends wanted to go for a beer, he thought it was normal and
understandable that she forgot to call and tell him that she would
not be there.

Though annoying, his mother's neglect of his feelings seemed
normal to him. He occasionally thought about complaining, but
he reminded himself that bringing up these topics most often leads
to more lashing out. So, he tolerated this mistreatment for years,
even though things got steadily worse. By age forty-six, after twenty
years of marriage, he realized he was miserable. At this point,
he decided it was too late to do anything about it. A part of him
also still believed that being treated this way was normal and there
was nothing else out there for him. So, he lived the rest of his life
depressed and miserable.

Freeing yourself from a life of trauma and abuse requires that you
increase your awareness and sensitivity to decrease your tolerance of
being mistreated. Whenever even minor forms of mistreatment occur in
relationships, they need to be addressed immediately. The relationship
needs to either be modified or ended. The damage done by tolerating
the repeated mistreatment of others is more than just the pain you feel
or dissociate to avoid feeling. The deeper damage is to your self-esteem
and self-definition. By tolerating mistreatment, you define yourself as
someone not worthy of respect. You feel helpless against bullies and not
entitled to being treated with respect and affection by others. People
pleasing develops as an effort to serve others in order to earn crumbs of

affection or respect as compensation for feeling worthless. You allow yourself to be treated as worthless.

In the next chapter, you will learn how to take back your sense of worth and self-respect. This will prepare you for part 3 of this book, where I guide you through resuming your personal growth and taking control of your self-definition and your environment.

Chapter 7

Emotional
Reprocessing

In chapter 6, you learned how to identify symptoms of childhood trauma that have followed you into adulthood. I gave you tools to help neutralize dissociation and regression. You will need to use these tools consistently as you need to be fully present to benefit from emotional reprocessing. This process will give you the chance to take back parts of you that were attacked, distorted, or denied by your parent.

It is not your parent that you will take yourself back from. You are in you, undeveloped or underdeveloped, hiding from you. Childhood experiences are recorded and understood as a child would. These memories and understanding of these events tend to be simplistic and impressionistic, which is how the child's brain functions. In your situation, the persistent lying and gaslighting created substantial distortions that were convincing to the traumatized child that was you. Emotional reprocessing involves revisiting every aspect of your childhood memories and understanding them from the adult perspective that you now have access to.

You will likely find this part of your healing unsettling. You will discover wounds that you didn't know you had. You will remember events and conversations you have not thought of for many years. You will become aware of things that should have happened, but didn't.

Some of these recollections will come during periods of intentional introspection. Many will pop into your mind when you are thinking of something else, or nothing at all. Some memories will come into your dreams.

I assure you: You can handle facing these things. Anyone who survives an abusive childhood and has the strength and intelligence to seek guidance toward healing and growth can surely tolerate the discomfort of the healing process. You have gained incredible strength for having survived abuse. You were probably gaslighted into feeling weak. You were called ungrateful, evil, or a loser. You felt broken, weak, and damaged, but you are stronger than you know. Your parent was threatened and intimidated by your strength and that drew frequent attacks, but you survived. Similar to physical wounds, scar tissue is stronger than virgin skin. You have tools now that you didn't have before and I will give you more tools in the coming chapters.

You will probably experience many memories and insights as "popping into your mind." It may seem like they come out of nowhere but they are actually the product of complex neurological processes, many of which you are not consciously aware of. Your brain processes information twenty-four hours each day, most of which you are not aware of, but you can become aware of. Cognitive processes that you are not aware of are passive in the sense that you don't intentionally seek understanding or problem solving. To reprocess this information, you must bring it into your awareness. You do this by converting the passive process into an active process. You do this by taking each of these memories and questioning them.

The questions that you ask yourself should be designed to examine two points of inquiry. The first is to examine the accuracy and validity of your recollections. This is necessary not only because these memories and impressions were recorded by a child but also because there was likely lying and gaslighting from your parent intentionally designed to distort your memory. The second focus of inquiry is to understand the context of your memories for the purpose of constructing a more accurate narrative. In other words, you need to get the story straight not only for accuracy of memory but also to understand the story from an adult perspective.

Clarifying Distorted Images of Yourself in the Broken Mirror

The first and most important subject of your emotional reprocessing is your understanding of who you are. This process will help you to take yourself back. You will find the truth about who you are and who you were meant to be as the gaslight smoke clears from your mind. Jerry's story is an example of the beginning of this process.

Jerry's Story

I always felt like a disappointment in my father's eyes. He was always telling me what I was doing wrong and correcting me. I didn't hold my pencil right. I didn't draw well. I was not good at athletics. I used to feel bad for him that he didn't have a son he was proud of. I kept trying to please him, but I always seemed to fall short.

My father used to do side jobs on the weekends to make extra money. When I turned eight years old, he started bringing me with him on the weekends. At first, I was very excited that he wanted to be with me. He told me I needed to learn to work with my hands so I could support myself someday. We built decks, replaced windows, and sometimes did repairs in people's homes.

For forty-eight years, I have been trying to make up for not being smart. I learned early in my life that if you are not born smart or with some talent, you have to work extra hard just to keep up. I dropped out of high school when I was sixteen because I knew college was not an option: when I was in tenth grade, my father told me that he only had enough money to send one kid to college and he was saving it for my sister who was "smart like her mother." So, I apprenticed as an assistant plumber when I was eighteen and I am now a licensed plumber. I have my own shop and make a good living. Anyone can learn to be a plumber and make money if they are willing to work hard enough.

I was recently approached by a contractor I work with named Raul. He asked me to design a plumbing system for a commercial project. The job paid more than I ever dreamed of making, but I have never done anything like this before. I told him the job was over my head and that he should find someone smarter and more capable. He looked at me with a funny look on his face and said, "You are one of the smartest people I know. If you can't design and build this system, nobody can."

I was shocked by what this man said to me. I am not smart and I am not educated. Was this man playing me? How could anyone possibly see me as smart? I was truly baffled. I tried to look at myself as this other man saw me: smart. From our previous work together, he could see me as dependable. I always show up on time and get the work done when promised or before. He might see me as organized as I always had the right parts and the right tools to use.

Then I remembered that I used to solve plumbing problems for him. I found ways to put pipes and drains in small areas he could not figure out. I also helped him with a legal issue he had when one of his customers sued him. It just seemed like common sense at the time.

I started to look at myself differently after that. I remembered my second-grade teacher Ms. Moran telling me I should be in honors class. She said she would meet with my parents to discuss it. When my father came back from the meeting, he told me that I didn't qualify because the honors kids were much smarter than me and I would fail. He also told me I didn't want to be around "smarty pants" because they were all full of themselves and not good people. Anyone smarter than him was a jerk.

I also started to remember I used to like trivia contests, game shows, and crossword puzzles. My father scowled at me when he saw me doing these things. He discouraged me and told me that these activities were for "geeks" and I needed to learn to use my hands if I wanted to be able to support myself.

I realized my father was threatened by people smarter than him, especially men. So, he convinced me that not only was I not smart but also that it was not desirable to be smart because it was not manly. I also realized that I feel differently. I realized that I can feel differently. I am going to take the job designing the plumbing system. I think I can change my life.

Jerry had to look into the broken mirror in order to heal himself. He didn't even know the mirror was broken until Raul saw a totally different Jerry. Once Jerry realized his perception of himself and the associated feelings were based on his father's broken mirror, he was able to discover his true self: he had been smart all along, he initially was excited about education, and his father lied and gaslighted him because he could not tolerate having a son smarter than him. He projected his feelings of inferiority onto his son and gaslighted him into believing that being smart was not desirable for men.

Jerry was able to see that he was smart and that he could develop his knowledge and intelligence and still be the man he wanted to be. He reprocessed his feelings about being intelligent and about himself as an emotionally intelligent man.

Chapter 8 is devoted to reprocessing your perceptions and feelings about yourself. Jerry's story demonstrates this process. You are now ready to begin this process for yourself. Jerry's story involves only one image in his broken mirror that concerns intelligence. Your mirror is full of images of the many different qualities that make you who you are. Each image you reprocess will bring you closer to being the person you were meant to be. The best person you can be. And you will be rewarded with experiencing yourself as a whole person, well and authentic. Your life will change in ways you cannot yet imagine. It is not easy, but I will guide you.

Images of Others in the Broken Mirror

It is not only your sense of self that needs emotional reprocessing because of the broken mirror (although it is the most important). The broken mirror is also filled with distorted images of your family, friends, teachers, and others who were part of your social world growing up. The strong tendency for individuals who suffer from symptoms of BPD to see others in idealized and devalued terms leads them to aggrandize people they like and disparage those they don't. As you recall, review, and rediscover the childhood that you got through more or less dissociated, you will notice that your parent consistently judged people and developed strong impressions about them. Your parent probably makes it clear to others and anyone who will listen to what they think or feel about people in their life. The instability and transactionality associated with BPD often result in reclassification based on recent events, usually in these terms:

- Anyone significant, especially family members, was seen as wonderful or awful. Others are considered wonderful when they cooperate with your parent and give them goods or services or feed their ego. Nonetheless, wonderful people would become horrible people if they failed to cooperate or acquiesce.

- Everyone else is devalued. You probably recall that there was a group of people, often relatives, that were consistently spoken about in negative terms. Even the mention of these individuals probably elicited a negative comment from your parent, often accompanied by a scowl or an eye roll. You were discouraged from seeing these people, speaking to them on the telephone, or even mentioning them in conversation. You might have been punished if you did. You were told these individuals, who failed to please your parent in some way, were pariahs, evil, etc. Naturally, you would assume that these individuals have nothing to offer you or that they would be negative influences in your life.

- Anyone can be put on the persona non grata list. It is very common for grandparents, uncles, aunts, cousins, and other family members to be on this list. Neighbors and friends might be on the list. Most disturbingly, spouses might be on that list. This includes both their spouse and yours.

You will come to discover that not everything your parent said about some of these people was true. Cheri figured this out too late.

Cheri's Story

Cheri, now forty-five, loves her father, but always felt uncomfortable around him. She liked to be with him at family events, but avoided being alone with or confiding in him with her personal life and feelings. She had felt this way all her life and it felt normal to her.

A friend of hers, Gwen, lost her father and asked Cheri to go to the funeral. Gwen was devasted by her loss and was very grateful Cheri agreed to go to the funeral. Cheri was struck by her friend's grief at her loss. Cheri had lost her father two years before. Cheri recalled feeling numb and detached at her father's funeral. She wondered what her dad had done to her to make her feel awkward and uncomfortable throughout her childhood. No matter how hard she tried, she could not remember a single incident of his being inappropriate or aggressive with her.

What she did remember was her mother frequently acting as though her father was not safe to be around. She would not allow her father to tuck her into bed when she was young or bathe her. Her mother would get visibly upset when her father tried to hug or kiss her. Her mother also frequently made innuendos about her father being sexually insatiable and even questioned her father's fidelity in conversations with Cheri during her adolescence. Her mother also warned her of her father's temper and how she was afraid of him.

Cheri clearly remembered her mother's depiction of her father as being dangerous and inappropriate, but she could not remember anything of what her mother described from her own observations. She did not remember him raising his voice toward her or her mother. Or anyone else. She did not remember being touched inappropriately by her father nor did remember him as being intrusive.

The more Cheri tried to remember what her father had done to push her away, the more she remembered how gentle and loving he was. Cheri also thought about how others, women in particular, were around her father. She remembered that women were generally comfortable around her father. They were relaxed and open, but respectful of him being a married man and a father. She realized that the only one who actually had a problem with her father was her mother and that she had adopted her mother's perspective. A view that her mother repeated and reinforced whenever her mother could find the opportunity.

Cheri came to realize that her mother created a devalued image of her father because her mother wanted to be the preferred parent. She was threatened by the possibility that Cheri and her father would be close and she would be left out, so she alienated herself from her father. This left Cheri with many feelings about her relationship with her father that she needed to reprocess.

She realized that her father was not lecherous. He loved her and had to walk on eggshells around his wife to show it. He was afraid to show affection because he did not want to be accused of being a predator. Cheri had thought he did not care about her or that he was struggling with inappropriate feelings toward her. She now realized that her father loved her the way Gwen's father loved Gwen, but he was afraid to show it. It broke Cheri's heart when she realized that she had missed the opportunity to be close to her father, who wanted to be close to her. She pushed him away and avoided him due to her mother's misinformation.

As she continued to emotionally reprocess the events of childhood and associated feelings, she came to understand that her mother's misinformation not only inhibited her attachment to her father but also to men in general. This is why she had thus far been unable to trust a man enough to have a long-term intimate relationship. Over the years, many of her boyfriends had told her she was hard to get close to. She had thought that they were just trying to manipulate her. When she discussed this with her mother, her mother reinforced to Cheri that men are aggressive and exploitative. Her mother was still discouraging her from being close to others because she wanted to hold onto Cheri and maintain primary access. Cheri also realized her mother had encouraged her to see herself as a sex object to men, who are fundamentally indiscriminate, and that she had little value as a companion or partner. It hadn't occurred to her that men would value her for who she is—and not just a sex object.

The emotional reprocessing described above was at times very painful to Cheri, but it offered tremendous opportunities for healing and growth. Her ability to attach to men had been damaged by her mother's lying and misrepresentations. Understanding this allowed her to heal her damaged attachment ability, grow as a woman and partner, and experience healthy intimacy. It also allowed her to heal her damaged self-image of being desirable only as a sex object. This afforded her the opportunity to grow in her understanding of herself and the development of personal qualities that offer confidence in her pursuing intimacy.

Sadly, Cheri's father did not live long enough for her to allow him to be close to her in the way he wanted. She mourned the loss of the opportunity, but was able to reprocess experiencing past events with the realization that her father always looked at her with feelings of love, honor, and pride. She came to realize that these reconstructions of past events were more accurate than her original perceptions that were tainted by her mother's projections. She felt closer to him now than when he was still alive. It was almost like a second chance.

Both Jerry and Cheri grew up believing the lies and distortions in the broken mirror constructed by their parents. They ignored their own experiences, thoughts, and judgments and took the lies of their parents as their truths. Jerry ignored, or discounted, his strength in problem solving and his second-grade teacher Ms. Moran recommending him for honors class. His father led him to believe it was an error and he accepted this without question. Cheri accepted her mother's narrative about her father and took it to be her own, even though her experience with her father was not consistent. Both Jerry and Cheri denied their own reality, perception, and judgment and adopted the perspective of their parents. Jerry's feelings about his own intelligence and Cheri's feelings about her father were determined by a distortion of the reality supplanted by their parents to meet their own needs.

Chapter 9 is devoted to helping you reclaim relationships from the past and creating a healthy social network going forward. You will have to go through the process Cheri went through with each of your relationships. Hopefully, many of those individuals you have become estranged from are still alive and available to heal the relationship with you. In most cases, the people you were alienated from in childhood know that your parent has discouraged your relationship with them, but they were powerless to do anything about it. When you approach them with the offer of healing and growth, they are extremely likely to welcome this opportunity.

Images That Bias Your Ability to Think Clearly in the Broken Mirror

Like Jerry and Cheri, you were probably groomed to accept the perceptions and judgments of others over your own when they conflict. Parents suffering from symptoms of BPD are generally extremely reluctant to acknowledge if they are wrong or have made an error. Doing so makes them feel flawed or defective. Acknowledging, even to themselves, that their child is right about something that they were wrong about is intolerable. For this reason, parents with symptoms of BPD teach their children from the youngest age that when they have a different observation, opinion, reaction, or judgment than the parent, they are always wrong. The child is always wrong. This is often reinforced by the parent by punishing or lashing out at the child when they dare to even suggest that they might be correct and the parent is wrong.

If you were raised in a household where from childhood you were always wrong, even when objective evidence suggests otherwise, you probably have generalized that to all other relationships. This probably causes you to experience significant self-doubt and to seek the validation and confirmation of others to assure you that your perceptions and judgments are accurate. You have been taught not to trust yourself. This leaves you extremely vulnerable to being misled, lied to, and gaslighted by others trying to manipulate you. You are always at a disadvantage in relationships with others because they are right when you disagree.

This is an example of the deepest and most destructive levels of damage caused by lying and gaslighting through the broken mirror. This level involves distortion beyond the level of what you think about to the level of how you think. As was the case for Jerry and Cheri, damage caused by being lied to and gaslighted by a parent can lead to significantly dysfunctional behavior in important or all relationships. This causes you to approach social situations with a bias. In almost all cases, the bias puts you at a disadvantage. Mira's childhood is another example.

Mira's Story

Mira was raised by a parent with symptoms of BPD who let her know from her early childhood that it was not okay to tell her things that would displease her. Mom was not subtle about letting her know. When someone said something that made Mom unhappy, she lashed out and or punished whoever spoke.

Her mother reacted hurtfully when criticized, challenged, or contradicted. Mira remembered trying everything she could do to avoid setting her mother off, but the list of topics Mom reacted to seemed endless. Even a comment to Mom or in her presence suggesting that Mom spilled something or forgot to mail a letter would trigger aggression. Each time Mom lashed out at her, Mira remembered the topic as one to avoid speaking to Mom about.

As Mira got older, she realized that the list of topics that Mom responded hurtfully to included talking about incidents or individuals that Mom did not like. Any expression of an opinion that her mother did not agree with resulted in lashing out. She also realized that her mother also reacted hurtfully when Mira expressed her feelings to her. When Mira expressed feeling badly, her mother took that as a criticism of her mother's parenting and lashed out, often blaming Mira for causing her own pain or discomfort. When Mira expressed good feelings, such as pride, well-being, or accomplishment, Mom became jealous and made hurtful comments suggesting that Mira's well-being was the result of Mira being a neglectful child.

Sharing with her mother that she was feeling ill also went badly. On one occasion, Mira had food poisoning and was experiencing vomiting and diarrhea for forty-eight hours. Her mother insisted Mira take a laxative. Doing this made Mira feel worse. Her mother insisted that she continue to take the laxative and became enraged when Mira refused. She then complained each time Mira vomited that Mira was spreading her illness to the whole family and made Mira clean the bathroom herself. Similarly, when Mira had bronchitis, her mother yelled at her for coughing too loudly and ruining her sleep.

Mira and her family joined together to create an environment that wouldn't trigger Mom's anger and hurtful behavior. They all walked on eggshells and blamed each other when she was set off. Even other relatives learned to tiptoe around Mom; doing so was normalized in her family.

Mira generalized her need to walk on eggshells to all of her relationships. This resulted in her being anxious in almost all social situations. She was timid in relationships and was very guarded about raising topics with others. She rarely expressed her feelings, preferences, or opinions because she was fearful of saying something that others would not like and then suffering their wrath.

The effects of Mira being taught to think this way about relationships had devastating effects on her functioning and sense of well-being. She never approached bosses for raises because she was afraid that they would be angry with her for doing so. She avoided asking others for help because she was afraid that they would feel burdened and lash out at her. She was even reluctant to ask a person who was inadvertently hurting her to make an adjustment: She once stood on a train for forty minutes with someone's elbow in her ribs because she did not want them to be angry at her.

Her aversion to expressing her feelings to others left her feeling very lonely. She did not share feelings with her friends and never asked for anything. She felt isolated most of the time. She even was reluctant to tell her doctors when something was bothering her. She thought her doctor would blame her for being hurt or injured and felt like she was bothering the doctor by seeking medical care.

Mira's love life was also profoundly affected. She was very anxious in intimate relationships because she always anticipated that her partner or paramour would get angry at her for something she might say. She became a people pleaser in an effort to keep romantic partners happy or placated so they wouldn't lash out. Healthy individuals were turned off by the one-sidedness of the relationship as Mira didn't share feelings or opinions. Exploitive individuals were fine with the one-sidedness, but these relationships were unsatisfying to Mira. By the time she was thirty, she stopped seeking out intimacy with others and accepted chronic loneliness.

When Mira was thirty-six, her father got untreatable advanced cancer. Her mother found taking care of him too stressful, so Mira stayed by his side as he declined. Shortly before he passed on, her father apologized to Mira. He confessed he was too afraid of Mira's mother to do anything but stand aside and let her do whatever she wanted to do. He apologized to Mira for not protecting her and allowing her to be exploited by her mother.

Mira then began reprocessing the message of the broken mirror. It took her years of looking at relationships and questioning why it was alright for others to express themselves without fear, but that anything she expressed might incite wrath. That she was entitled to her opinions and her needs and that if others were offended by these expressions, there was something wrong with them and not her. She continued to be thoughtful and respectful of others, as this was her nature, but she started taking some risks and asking for help, attention, or cooperation when needed.

At first, she was very surprised that others actually wanted to hear what she had to say, even if she did not agree with them. She was even more surprised that healthy people appreciated the opportunity to help her or do things for her when she offered them that opportunity. She also realized that people who only wanted to hear what they wanted were not candidates for intimacy.

In this chapter, I introduced you to the most valuable tool for your healing and growth: seeing the broken mirror as broken and then revisiting, or reliving, past experiences as they should have been experienced if you had an accurate mirror. You will have to identify the persistent lies and gaslighting of your parent with symptoms of BPD and then imagine how your life would have been if your parent had been honest and supportive. This will open a door to the future that up until now you might not have known exists.

Note that in the examples offered in this chapter, Jerry, Cheri, and Mira each identified one image in the broken mirror and profoundly benefited from the reprocessing. For Jerry, one image had to do with his intellect; for Cheri, it was her relationship with her father; and for Mira, it was that she needed to walk on eggshells to get along with others. Your optimal recovery will be that you identify and process multiple distortions that came through the broken mirror. Chapter 8 will focus on distortions in your sense of self and self-image that need to be reprocessed and reclaimed. Chapter 9 will focus on distortions in your relationships. In chapter 10, I will show you how your thinking was distorted and how through emotional reprocessing you will learn how to think more objectively and utilize the full power of your mind and your intelligence.

You are now well on your way!

Part 3

Growth

Chapter 8

Reclaiming the Self That Was Meant to Be

Now that you are on your way to healing chronic and traumatic wounds, you are ready to unleash the processes of personal growth that were inhibited or arrested by an abusive childhood. Parents who suffer from symptoms of BPD are threatened by their children's growth, autonomy, and independence, so they inhibit their children's growth in obvious and covert ways.

The desire to sabotage your personal growth is driven by the parent's fear of abandonment, which is a core symptom of BPD. Their efforts to sabotage your growth can not only be intentional but also are often not in their awareness. Like a person drowning in the ocean, they will grab onto anything that looks like it can support them. Unskilled rescuers have been known to be victims of double drowning when they are frantically grabbed around the head and forced under the water. You must not allow this to happen to you anymore. ACOB2 experienced sabotage throughout his childhood, but because of the gaslighting, did not realize he was being sabotaged until he was well into adulthood.

ACOB2: Actual Child of a Parent with BPD Symptoms

It was extremely confusing. I grew up in New York City and went to the local public elementary school. My mother had always stressed the importance of learning and getting good grades. She was a teacher by profession. I was a good student and many of my teachers encouraged me.

At the end of sixth grade, as I was preparing for graduation, I also prepared to move on to the local public intermediate school. While I had a good experience in the public elementary school, I had heard rumors that the intermediate school was less academic and less safe. I heard some of my friends talking about going to different intermediate schools and asked my mother if this was an option for me. She told me that the other schools were private schools, I could not go because they were too far away, and we couldn't afford it.

I was very disappointed. Other kids could go to private school, but I couldn't. I figured maybe the other kids lived closer and had fathers that could pay for it. My father was estranged. One day, my sixth-grade teacher asked me if I was going to take the test to get into private school. I told her that I was not going to because my family lived too far away and that my family could not afford it, so there was no reason for me to take the test. She explained to me that the city would provide me with a bus pass and the school would offer a scholarship if I scored high on the test.

I took the test and was offered admission to two very highly regarded prep schools, but no scholarship was offered. I asked my mother if I could go without a scholarship; she said no. My teacher asked if I had gotten into any schools and I told her that I did, but I could not go because I did not get a scholarship. She asked me if my mother had submitted a financial aid form. I asked my mother—she said she had not. I asked her why—she told me that the form was too complicated for her and she didn't know how to fill it out.

I asked my grandmother to help her with the financial aid form. Shortly after, the form was submitted. I eagerly awaited their decision and was heartbroken when they still did not offer financial aid. At this point, a friend in the family (also a teacher) asked to see the financial aid form my mother had submitted. She had reported that she made ten times what her actual income was for the year before. We got this corrected and the school offered me a full scholarship.

My mother claimed that she was "bad with numbers," even though she was a licensed schoolteacher. Other family members confirmed: "Your mother is not good with stuff like that." I believed them.

Until it came up again when I was a senior in high school. Mother wanted me to go to a local college so that I could continue to live at home while going to college. The local college was private and I was concerned about tuition costs. She assured me that money had been put away for me to go to college, so I should apply. I didn't want to go to the local college so I applied to colleges upstate and got in. This time, I completed the financial aid form myself. I had to ask her for her income data three times, but she was "bad with numbers," so it was understandable.

During the first semester of college, she took every opportunity to abuse during telephone calls. She said I abandoned her and I was a horrible person just like my father. I was so upset by these calls, I was unable to study. After a weak first semester, I stopped the calls so that I could function. When I started receiving tuition bills, I asked her for the money saved for me for school. She told me to take on loans and she would give me the money after I graduated. When I graduated, she told me that she had no money.

It was twenty years later that I realized my mother sabotaged my efforts to educate myself because she wanted me to stay home

and take care of her. I remembered I had to fill out my college
applications at the local McDonald's because she continuously
disrupted me while I was working. I was understanding at first
because I knew that we had little money and had to live in a small
apartment. Upon reflection, I realized that the apartment was
quiet when she needed to work, but not when I did.

I later came to realize she had gaslighted me and the rest of the
family into believing that she was bad with numbers and that's why
I almost missed out on some wonderful educational opportunities.
I needed to separate myself from her to grow.

Identifying Areas Where Personal Growth Is Inhibited

Personal development is not a single dimension. Each aspect of your personality is its own dimension. It is very common for the growth of the dimensions to occur at different rates. Parts of you may be very mature, while other parts of yourself are very immature. For example, someone can be very mature with finances or parenting while at the same time be reckless with road rage.

The first step in reclaiming your sense of self by restoring natural growth processes is to identify which areas have been stunted, where your growth has been inhibited. There are two ways to approach this and you should do both. The first method is to look at your own behavior in all situations and ask yourself if the behavior is more adult-like or more childlike. Is cursing at other drivers while driving your car adult-like? Is overeating or drinking too much adult-like? You should also ask yourself what adult-like behaviors or decisions look like when you are frustrated or seeking enjoyment.

The second method for identifying areas of yourself that are underdeveloped is experiential. This involves asking yourself how it feels when you make decisions or engage in behaviors. Does it feel adult-like to avoid situations, like asking your manager for a raise because it makes you uncomfortable? Selma experienced this when her friend Brea forgot to invite her to her daughter Jade's third birthday party. They had the following conversation:

Brea: *Hi, Selma. We missed you at the birthday party.*

Selma: *I wasn't invited.*

Brea: *OMG. You didn't get the invitation?*

Selma: *No.*

Brea: *You knew about the party. Why didn't you just come over?*

Selma: *I don't go to parties that I am not invited to.*

Brea: *Of course, you were invited. The post office probably lost it.*

Selma: *I felt like you didn't want me there.*

Brea: *We have always been together for Jade's milestones. She calls you Aunt Sel.*

Selma felt very childish during this interaction. She felt like a little girl being spoken to by a coach who didn't start her for a soccer game because she cried and sulked. She thought about the possibility that her invitation was sent but did not arrive, but was too uncomfortable to ask Brea before the party. She ended up missing out.

Understanding How You Got Stuck

Once you identify underdeveloped areas of thought, feelings, or behaviors, you need to understand what has stopped you from naturally growing. Ask yourself what an adult-like response to any given situation would be and then ask yourself why you are uncomfortable or unable to act like an adult.

Road rage is a common example. Yelling in the car at someone who can't hear you, attempting to provoke another driver with lewd gestures, or dangerous driving are childish reactions to frustration. Most adults reflecting on this behavior would be able to see that it is childish and counterproductive. Most adults can understand that a more mature response would be to yield to aggressive drivers and stay clear of them, rather than provoking them. A likely cause of choosing to act out road rage is that it was experienced as a personal slight or defeat. Further consideration can lead to added insight that road rage is not personal. In almost all cases, the aggressive driver is a stranger, so it could not be personal. This understanding will increase the likelihood that a more mature response will be comfortable and natural in a road rage situation.

As Selma reflected on her exchange with Brea, she realized that when she did not receive the invitation to Jade's birthday party, she either should have asked Brea about it or just showed up. As she imagined herself acting adult-like, she realized she did not have enough confidence to comfortably behave that way. She eventually identified a pattern of childlike behavior when confidence is needed to act maturely. As she reflected on her childhood, she realized that her father, who had symptoms of BPD, always made her feel like she was doing the wrong thing. He always knew better than her and he let her know whenever he could. When they disagreed, he was never wrong. Nobody could develop confidence under those circumstances.

Selma might also have discovered that in ambiguous situations, she tended to assume the worst. In the example of Jade's birthday party, it was ambiguous whether getting an invitation was intentional or accidental. The assumption that she was not invited made it a fait accompli; it yielded the result she dreaded. Similarly, avoiding asking one's manager for a raise becomes a fait accompli because you will not get a raise. You determine the worst outcome by anticipating it.

Restarting Your Growth Process

Once you have identified areas where your personal growth was stunted and come to understand the obstacles to growth, you need to remove those obstacles to restart the natural growth process.

Selma discovered that her personal growth was stunted by her coping with difficult situations by avoiding them. She avoided them because she lacked confidence in her likability and her decisiveness. From her conversation with Brea, it was clear that if she followed her initial instinct to ask her about the invitation when she did not receive it, her inclination was correct and asking Brea about the invitation would have succeeded in getting her invited. She realized that she had good judgment, but was afraid to act on it because her father had told her over and over again that she was always wrong.

To restart her personal growth process, Selma will have to take some risks. She will have to trust her instincts in ambiguous situations and resist her tendency to avoid uncomfortable situations so she can build confidence in her capabilities and self-worth. If Selma persists with this process of reclaiming parts of herself, uncomfortable situations will become opportunities to continue her personal growth rather than occasions to act childishly and avoid difficult adult transactions. For example, the frequent attacks on Selma's confidence by her father might inhibit her asking for a raise or promotion at work or her willingness to date. Over time, she will be rewarded with greater confidence and self-esteem, which will help her optimize her ability to function successfully in every endeavor. She will become the adult that she was meant to be. She will feel like a confident and successful adult rather than a weak frighted little child who is always wrong.

If you have never engaged in a rigorous process of self-examination and self-reflection, this process may seem daunting to you. As the child of a parent with symptoms of BPD, you were probably discouraged from self-reflection throughout your life. You were trained to focus on the feelings of others, not your own. You may have been punished for expressing your feelings to your parent. Many individuals in this circumstance avoid self-reflection as they stare into the broken mirror; they go numb to their own feelings. They just take direction from others. This creates a selfless people pleaser. You need to go through this to be free. And once you do, you will never look back.

The remainder of this chapter will describe common areas of stunted growth in adult children of parents with symptoms of BPD. This will provide a starting point for your journey to reclaim the person you were meant to be. With each fragment that you reclaim, your sense of well-being will increase noticeably. Your efforts will be well compensated.

Where to Start

Your parent's efforts to inhibit your growth are driven by their fear of abandonment. Young children are weak and dependent. The total helplessness and constant neediness that is natural with infants and toddlers offers the parent constant reassurance that they are of value to the child and that the child will not leave. You could not leave.

Children naturally seek to exercise tools of independence as soon as they develop. They naturally prefer to feed themselves, dress themselves, and choose their activities. Healthy parents encourage their children to maximize independence and celebrate their children's ability to provide for themselves. In contrast, parents with symptoms of BPD are threatened by their children's self-sufficiency. They worry that when you can walk, you will walk away. When you can choose who to be with, you will not choose them. Like trimming a bonsai tree, they prevent you from reaching for the sun by inhibiting your growth in that direction.

This is where you begin. You identify the aspects of yourself that would most likely be threatening to a parent trying to hold onto their child forever. The elements of healthy growth. Here are some common areas:

- Self-confidence

- Self-esteem

- Self-awareness

- Power

I will now show you how to reclaim undeveloped or distorted aspects of yourself, once you identify them. The core process we will be using is emotional reprocessing. Reclaiming your self-confidence will help you reclaim other aspects of yourself, so it is the best place to start.

Signs of Damaged Self-Confidence

- Do you have difficulties making decisions on your own?

- Do you question your own judgment?

- Do you let others make decisions for you?

- Do you question your competence?

- Are you intimidated by new situations and challenges?

- Do you avoid them?

- Do you expect to fail?

If you experience one or more of these symptoms regularly, you probably have damaged or underdeveloped self-confidence. You may have been experiencing it for so long that you didn't even recognize it. You might have normalized it. This is a natural result of being told consistently by your parent that you are wrong about everything and always to blame. The result of being lied to and gaslighted by the person you trusted the most. They projected their fear of being flawed onto you and you came to believe them. Your growth was inhibited by your parent frequently reminding you that you are not capable of taking care of yourself and making good decisions.

Now that you have identified areas where your personal growth was obstructed and identified how this is affecting you today, you need to subject each of these areas to rigorous reexamination. Your examination of the self-confidence you would have developed if you grew up in a supportive environment should involve three different viewpoints:

1. **Objective view:** This view reveals what really happened throughout your childhood. It involves identifying facts and beliefs that were distorted because of lying and gaslighting. Much like a detective, you need to seek clarity about your past by collecting data about your childhood. Speaking to friends and relatives who knew you as a child will be very helpful. Photos, recordings, diaries, and notes all facilitate this process.

2. **Subjective view:** This is what you thought was happening at the time. In many instances, your conceptualization of what was happening was childlike. In areas where your growth was stunted, you are still thinking about these things from a childish perspective. You are probably thinking about yourself in childish ways.

3. **Projected view:** The projected view is the way your parent wanted you to see things. This is determined by a combination of how you were spoken to and how you were treated.

Now you can examine the three viewpoints from an adult perspective. This will result in the creation of a new narrative of old events. You will be able to see your childhood from an adult perspective and you will understand things you could not understand as a child. You will understand how the broken mirror derailed healthy development and damaged your self-esteem.

Once you construct and accept the narrative of your childhood from an adult perspective, you can react to what happened as an adult. You emotionally reprocess your childhood from an adult perspective, which resumes the process of personal growth and allows you to reclaim the parts of yourself that were meant to be. You will actualize your potential by transforming your self-concept from a childish one—based on the distortions of the broken mirror—to an adult one—based on the truth. In the following example, Kelly realizes she was seeing herself through a broken mirror. Using emotional reprocessing to reclaim her self-esteem changed her life.

Kelly's Story

Kelly is a thirty-two-year-old waitress at a diner. She has been working there for ten years and she is very well-liked by the manager as well as the clientele. She is very good at what she does. She is kind, courteous, and attentive and she always gets her orders right. She works very hard to support herself.

Over the years, many people have asked her what her ambitions were for the future. She would just shrug her shoulders. A few of the customers even offered her opportunities. One man was opening a franchise and asked her if she would like to apply as an assistant manager. She said she would think about it, but never got back to him.

Kelly was uncomfortable thinking about the future. She knew how to do what she was doing, but was afraid that she would fail at new challenges. This is why she didn't go to college even though her counselor encouraged her to apply as her grades were so good in high school.

She grew up with a parent who was constantly critical of her. Whatever Kelly did, her mother found something that would have made it better. As far back as she could remember, her mother would readjust her clothing, her hair, and her room. Her mother always commented on her studies and how she could do better. When Kelly went to her junior prom, her mother told her, "You look beautiful. Of course, you would be a real knockout if you lost a few pounds." One time, she mentioned to her mother that people had encouraged her to advance her career or get training and her mother responded, "What's wrong with the job you have?" Kelly had almost all of the signs of low self-confidence listed above.

One night, as she was closing the diner for the day with her manager, he asked her, "Why are you so unsure of yourself?" She was shocked by this comment. She never thought of herself as someone unsure of herself, but as soon as the words came out of his mouth, she realized it was true. She treats herself and presents herself like someone without confidence. Most strikingly, she realized she felt like someone of marginal competence and was afraid to take on challenges for fear of failure. She always felt this way, but never labeled it or thought that maybe she didn't need to feel this way anymore.

She decided she needed to answer her manager's question. Not for him, but for her. She first looked at the objective view: Was she competent? What had she failed at? She couldn't come up with a single example. She was successful in high school. She adequately supports herself and admirably takes care of her home. She was everyone's favorite waitress.

Next, she looked at the subjective view. She feels incompetent and like a failure. She always feels this way. She also realized that these feelings were inconsistent with the objective reality that, despite her feelings, she generally succeeds at things that she applies herself to. Often, she excels.

To understand why her feelings are so disparate from her history of competent functioning, she had to look at the projective view: Her mother brought her up treating her as though she were incompetent. She judged everything Kelly did and always found fault with her.

Kelly wondered why her mother would treat her as incompetent when she was actually quite capable. She remembered that her mother frequently expressed fears of abandonment and *being alone. She often complained about friends and relatives who would choose to be with others rather than her and how she resented them for that. Until now, it didn't occur to her that her mother would feel the same about her. Now she understood that her mother didn't want her to feel confident and independent for fear that Kelly would leave her to pursue her own life. Her mother felt most secure when Kelly was needy and unsure of herself. Her mother used the broken mirror to keep her feeling that way.*

Examining her development through these three perspectives allowed Kelly to change her childish narrative of being incompetent, fearful, and reluctant to take on challenges to an adult narrative of a very capable person who was lied to and gaslighted to believe she was incompetent because her mother's need to hold onto her forever. Kelly had lost many years of opportunity to develop self-confidence and find her strengths and successes. She knew she had to take some risks and take on new challenges to find herself. Her competent self. The self she was meant to be.

Taking risks was uncomfortable at first, but she finally stepped up to it. She took a course at the local community college in business management. She was surprised when she got an A. She took some more courses and eventually got an associate's degree. She contacted the man from the diner who opened franchises and asked to be considered for the next opening as an associate manager. Today, she manages her own franchise and is looking to open a second. She now sees herself as an adult and has gone from stuck to soaring. She took that part of herself back.

Once you take back your self-confidence, you can utilize the same method of emotional reprocessing to reclaim other parts of yourself that were inhibited by growing up with the broken mirror. With each part you reclaim, you will feel more whole, more stable, and more mature.

Below are signs of other areas of damage to your development that you can apply this method to.

Signs of Damaged Self-Esteem

- Do you allow others to treat you with disrespect?

- Do you accept being treated unfairly?

- Are you reluctant to stand up for yourself?

- Do you find it hard to believe that others would care about you?

- Do you treat others better than you do yourself?

- Do you automatically put the needs of others before your own?

- Do you automatically put the feelings of others before your own?

- Are you reluctant to ask for favors from others because you don't feel worthy?

- Do you take better care of others than you take care of yourself?

Signs of Damaged Self-Awareness

- Do you ignore uncomfortable feelings?

- Do you use substances to dull your feelings?

- Do you go along with others because you do not feel like you have preferences?

- Do you feel numb most of the time?

- Do you feel awkward rather than happy when you get what you want?

- Do you dislike when others ask you how you feel?

- Do you always say "fine" when asked?

Signs of Damaged Power

- Do you allow others to make decisions for you?

- Do you avoid taking leadership positions?

- Do you consider yourself a follower?

- Do you wait for others to initiate conversations or activities?

- Do you keep your thoughts to yourself?

Each part that you reclaim will require new challenges and new risks. This type of stimulation is necessary for growth. You might not always succeed in your first endeavor. It takes time to leave behind childish methods such as avoidance and move forward in a consistent way, but you will get there if you persevere. It will change your life. Going through this process of emotional reprocessing over and over again will also make you immune to broken mirrors in the future. The more you know yourself, the less vulnerable to lying and gaslighting you will be. You will no longer mistake distorted images for the truth.

In this chapter, you learned how to use the method of emotional reprocessing to reclaim parts of yourself that were underdeveloped due to frequent exposure to the broken mirror; the persistent distortions projected by your parent with BPD. The broken mirror also reflects distortions in your relationships with others, including family members. In the next chapter, I will show you how to use emotional reprocessing to reclaim lost relationships and underdeveloped abilities to participate in relationships associated with being raised by a parent with BPD.

Chapter 9

Reclaiming Your Social Network

Healthy development of a social network is a critical part of personal growth. Because many parents with symptoms of BPD find social networks threatening to their attachment to their children, it is hence another area where they tend to discourage growth in their children. In this chapter, I will show you how to take your relationships to a level you probably never dreamed of. A level that your parent probably never reached and never wanted you to experience because they were afraid you would leave them.

As a child of a parent with symptoms of BPD, you were trained to approach relationships as a people pleaser. You were taught that the needs and desires of others come first. Your needs and wants come second, if at all. You were trained to accept transactional approaches to intimacy, which are unstable and insecure. You were expected to bond with a parent who lashes out at you, lies to you, and gaslights you on a regular basis. Following is a list of some effects of being raised this way that persist into adulthood if unaddressed.

- Difficulty or discomfort saying no to others

- Fear and/or discomfort in intimate situations

- Fear of rejection

- Fear of displeasing others

- Reluctance to express opinions or preferences out of fear of being rejected or ridiculed

- Difficulty or discomfort with assertiveness

- Difficulty or discomfort being the center of attention

- Feeling uncomfortable when praised

- Feeling the need to give to others more than they give you

- Difficulty or discomfort asking others for help

- Difficulty trusting others

- Difficulty or discomfort expressing your feelings to others

- Extreme sensitivity to the emotions of others

- Feeling panicked or unable to respond when confronted by others

- Rumination about conversations with others that did not go as expected

- Difficulty or discomfort ending unhealthy relationships

If you experience any of these symptoms to a significant degree, or a combination of these symptoms, your social functioning is not optimal and the quality of your social network is less than you deserve. Don't be surprised if you have been experiencing these feelings throughout your life but never thought of them as symptoms or something that you might improve on. You needed to learn to function in this way to survive a traumatic childhood. You were rewarded for functioning this way by a parent who was threatened by your health and growth.

Unleashing your growth in this area will require you to address distortions in the way you think about and approach relationships in general, the form, and then apply emotional reprocessing to specific relationships with people you may be partially or fully alienated from. Here are a few examples of how your childhood experiences have left you with childish approaches to relationships.

Transactional Relationships

Healthy intimate relationships are movies, not snapshots. The instability of mood and sense of self that individuals with symptoms of BPD suffer from prevents them from forming stable and secure attachments. Their emotional dysregulation causes them to behave impulsively with others when they are emotionally stimulated. When they are pleased or satisfied, they treat others kindly. But when they are frustrated or hurt, they lash out at others, often causing pain to others. The way they treat others depends on their feelings and moods.

Intimate relationships are very emotionally stimulating. This makes them particularly unstable. The impulsivity and associated unstable behavior of the parent allows them to focus only on the immediate, or here and now. They do not see other people, or relationships with other people, in context. This caused Charley great frustration in his relationship with his father.

Charley's Story

Charley grew up with a father who suffered from symptoms of BPD. His father consistently made him feel like he was not a good son; Charley tried very hard consistently to change his father's perception. For twenty-four consecutive years, he made his father a priority on Father's Day by taking him to dinner or buying him a present and a cake. Charley married last year and both he and his wife, Paula, honored his father on Father's Day. He was also with his father on his father's birthday and for other important events.

This year, Charley's wife wanted to honor her father on Father's Day and take him to his favorite restaurant. They decided they would take both of their fathers out together and honor them both. Paula's father was very happy with this arrangement, but Charley was worried that his father would not take it well. Charley had the following conversation with his father.

Charley: *Dad, Paula and I would like to take you to The Steak House for Father's Day dinner.*

Dad: *Why The Steak House?*

Charley: *That is Paula's father's favorite restaurant. We thought we would take both of you out.*

Dad: *What am I, an afterthought? Why doesn't Paula spend the day with her father while you spend the day with me?*

Charley: *Dad, I have been with you every Father's Day since I was a child.*

Dad: *Stop making excuses for being a selfish son and giving in to your demanding wife.*

Charley: *Can't you understand that I am married now?*

Dad: *I understand perfectly. You would rather be with him than me.*

Charley: *We want to honor both of you.*

Dad: *You honor me by dumping me? How did I raise such a loser?*

Charley: *You are putting me in a difficult position. Can't you just cooperate?*

Dad: *Why can't you? I wish you were never born.*

Charley's father was unhappy with the Father's Day plan and lashed out at Charley. As far as Charley's father was concerned, twenty-four years of loyalty were wiped out because Charley's father did not want to share his time with his father-in-law on Father's Day.

Charley was disappointed with his father's response, but not surprised. He knew that no matter how much he saw his father in the past, his father would respond hurtfully if he didn't get what he wanted on any given day. When his father was displeased, he almost always accused him of being selfish, and since Charley had been married, he also accused Charley of being weak with Paula.

Naturally, this was very painful for Charley. He kept trying harder and harder to please his father. Eventually, something would displease his father and all of Charley's efforts were erased. He started to wonder if his father was right. Maybe he was selfish and let Paula push him around. Maybe he was hurting his poor father because of his selfish wife.

The broken mirror shows Charley as an ungrateful and selfish child. This directly contradicts his sustained efforts to please his father. Charley yields to the transactional approach he was raised with and begins to view himself in transactional terms. He also brings transactionality into his marriage as he changes his feelings about his wife based on a transaction with his father that she did not even participate in. This causes him to build resentment toward her.

Go back to the first page of this chapter and review the symptoms I described to you associated with suboptimal social functioning and you will see that almost all of them can be attributed to being raised transactionally. Charley began to experience many of these discomforts in anticipation of his conversation with his father, and it went downhill from there.

If you were raised by a parent who could only relate to you transactionally, then you probably anticipate that others will relate to you in this way. This causes you to be a people pleaser and to experience anxiety in most, if not all, of your relationships. It undermines your ability to trust others and attach securely. Transactional relationships are childlike and immature. Children in a playground will lash out at a friend who takes their toy or turn on a merry-go-round. Healthy adults form stable relationships based on established patterns of treating each other with kindness and respect.

To reclaim your ability to have secure contextual relationships, you must learn to reject the transactional view of relationships and insist that others accept that past events affect current and future transactions. Without this understanding, you will not endeavor to share intimacy. Charley attempted to do this with his father when he brought up the history of his attending to his father on Father's Day, but his father ignored him and he dropped it. Had Charley known how to pursue intimacy with his father, he might have said to his father something like this:

"Dad, I have always honored you on Father's Day, and I continue to do so today. I am using this occasion to include you in the family that I am creating with Paula. Our hope is that you can embrace her father as an in-law and consider him an asset to your life. This will open up opportunities when your grandchildren come, if we are lucky. If you decide to decline this invitation, then I will have to divide my time between you and my father-in-law and I will see you less. This is your choice, not mine."

Hearing this from Charley might not change his father's mind, but hopefully, Charley can see his behavior as consistent with his history of honoring his father, even though the broken mirror reflects the opposite. Taking back your ability to have a secure relationship requires that you identify when mirrors are broken and then dismiss their image. Do not ruminate on them, like Charley did.

Competitive vs. Cooperative Relationships

Another aspect of Charley's dialogue with his father is that it portrays intimate relationships as fundamentally competitive and therefore unstable. Charley's father sees Paula's father as a threat to his relationship with Charley. He encourages Charley to see his marriage as competitive. Instead of seeing Charley's marriage as an opportunity to enlarge and enhance two families, he sees it as a threat. Instead of embracing the idea of welcoming others into his family, he polarizes the new family structure and in doing so weakens it.

Charley was not surprised by this. Growing up, his father always separated him from friends, colleagues, and even other family members. If he was unable to get Charley's attention, affection, or presence, he would always ask what Charley was doing that was more important than his father. If he told his father who he was seeing, his father would criticize that person whenever possible. He would commence a character assassination. He even did this with Charley's sister!

Dad: *Charley, I need you to pick me up tomorrow at
            7:30 a.m. at the car repair shop.*

Charley: *I am sorry, Dad. I can't get there until 9:30.*

Dad: *Why not?*

Charley: *I promised to take Joyce to the mall.*

Dad: *Tell your sister to get an Uber.*

Charley: *I promised her. She is meeting her friend there.*

Dad: *Your lazy sister and her friend are more important than
            my transportation?*

Charley: *She is depending on me.*

Dad: *She is a spoiled little princess. And her friend is just*
         using her for a ride.

As a result of being raised in a competitive and polarized family environment, Charley learned to keep his friends and family members separated. He rarely brought friends home because he didn't want them targeted for character assassination. He was very uncomfortable in groups. He always felt like an outsider, like a second choice. He was incredibly hurt when his high school friends had a reunion and didn't send him an invitation, until one of them called the night before and asked him why he didn't RSVP. Later that night, he found the Evite in his spam filter and realized that he was mistaken about being slighted.

Charley struggled in all relationships to feel comfortable and secure. He was always worried that others would find someone they liked better and dump him. Even in his marriage, he worried about Paula's loyalty and fidelity even though she never gave him a reason to. It was a source of friction whenever she wanted to spend time with her friends or take business trips.

Competitive behavior is the opposite of cooperative behavior. When you compete with someone else, you want them to lose. When you cooperate, you want them to win. They are not compatible. Competitive behavior in intimate relationships is destructive and immature. One of the most common examples is sibling rivalry; however, most healthy brothers and sisters grow out of it and become closer during adulthood. Healthy intimate relationships require consistently cooperative behavior. Reclaiming your ability to have stable, secure intimate relationships requires that you reject competitive behavior in intimate transactions. You must recognize that individuals who approach a relationship with you competitively are not candidates for intimacy.

To grow his ability to have mature intimate relationships, Charley has to accept that his relationship with his father is not intimate. His father is either not capable or not willing to behave cooperatively on a consistent basis. He needs to stop the people pleasing and self-sacrifice he uses to try to get others to be intimate and loving to him. He must deal with his father transactionally—that is all that his father is willing or able to offer. He must accept that many people like his father are not healthy enough or mature enough to have an intimate relationship with, and he must stop trying.

If you are looking for intimacy in transactional relationships, you need to stop. You will need to take some risks to accomplish this. You have to stop chasing intimacy with people pleasing and walking on egg-shells and be willing to do without relationships that do not meet your needs. You need to hold off on emotional intimacy until you find others who honor and respect you and feel privileged to be with you.

Trust

Healthy intimate relationships require trust. The experience of feeling secure in a relationship is a direct manifestation of your ability to trust that individual. Without trust, you will always be anxious. Trust is a product of consistently supportive behavior.

If your parent frequently lied to you, gaslighted you, and manipulated you with a broken mirror, how could you trust them? You couldn't, but you had to anyway. As a child, you were dependent on your parent for basic survival: food, shelter, education, medical care, etc. Like climbing a broken ladder or driving with defective brakes, relying on an untrustworthy parent brings persistent and significant anxiety.

As an adult, you must never put yourself in this position again. You can have transactions with untrustworthy people, but you cannot rely on them. You must always have a backup plan. You must prepare to engage your backup plan whenever necessary. For example, if you made arrangements with an untrustworthy person to pick you up, you should have the phone numbers of taxis or an active Uber account so you don't get stranded.

You will also have to take some risks with trust to jump-start your growth in social networking. In relationships that do warrant trust, you have to stop second-guessing and challenging your loved one. Charley needs to stop asking his wife where she is when she is not with him and stop worrying about her leaving him. He must trust himself to have chosen someone who has shown themselves to be trustworthy, be prepared to cope if he is wrong, and trust his ability to discern trustworthy individuals from untrustworthy ones. He must take risks to build up his confidence through experience. Lastly, he must immediately stop trying to trust individuals who have shown to be consistently untrustworthy.

Using Emotional Reprocessing to Repair Broken Relationships

In the first part of this chapter, I showed you how mature intimate relationships function and guided you through transitioning your social skills to adapt to this level of function. To fully reclaim your social network, you will have to repair relationships with others that have been damaged by a broken mirror. Not all relationships will be salvageable. Some might be damaged beyond the point of repair.

In chapter 7, where I introduced to you the concept of emotional reprocessing, I shared Cheri's story. She was alienated from her father by years of her mother's lying, gaslighting, and character assassination. It took her until her mid-forties to reprocess her image of him, but by that time, it was too late to substantially repair the relationship. Her father didn't live long enough. In the remainder of this chapter, you will learn how to repair relationships damaged by the broken mirror and prevent it from tainting new ones.

First, we build on one of the directives from an earlier part of this chapter: stop trusting people who are untrustworthy. If your parent has repeatedly lied to you and frequently sought to alienate you from friends and family utilizing character assassination, you can't trust what they say about the people in your life. You must not incorporate their memories, observations, or opinions.

Next, you must reformulate your images of others based on or influenced by a broken mirror. As you do this, keep in mind that individuals with symptoms of BPD often communicate their feelings utilizing projection. In addition to conveying distorted or fabricated stories about people they don't like; they also non-verbally convey their disdain. They scowl at the mention of those they feel threatened by. They utter tones of anger and disgust and portray themselves as victims to those they want you to shun. This almost caused Delilah to make the biggest mistake of her life.

Delilah's Story

My mother never liked the boys I brought home to meet her. She would start off nice to them, but once she got to know them, she became increasingly critical. She would always find fault. She wasn't rude to their faces, but as soon as they left, she would tell me all the things that she found wrong with them. The more time she spent with them, the more faults she would find. When she talked about them she would make a face that looked like she smelled something spoiled or putrid. She often rolled her eyes and her voice got raspy. She acted this way toward my girlfriends and even some neighbors, but it was most noticeable with the boys. So, I stopped bringing my friends around, especially the boys.

When Stu and I got serious, I began to dread when I would have to introduce him to her. Stu and I started talking about living together, so I knew the time was near. Stu wanted to meet my mom. He didn't understand my reluctance. We agreed to meet for brunch one Sunday. She was on her best behavior and Stu still did not understand my reluctance. When Mom and I got home, the criticisms started immediately.

"Where did you find this guy? Does he always look so disheveled?" "Didn't his parents teach him manners?" "He seems like all the other bums you spend your time with; self-absorbed." "Why are you settling for someone so plain?" "Did you notice how he chews with his mouth open?"

When she realized that I was serious about Stu, her attacks became more pointed.

"Stu is only looking for sex. Once he gets what he wants, he will treat you like trash." "This guy you're with is going nowhere. You will regret marrying him." "Stu hates me. He will break up our family." "Don't trust this man. He is obviously a liar." "Do you see the way he looks at other women?"

Even though I knew she always spoke badly about my boyfriends, it started to get under my skin. I had trouble sleeping because I kept hearing her words over and over again in my ears. I started to have thoughts and images of Stu with other women and feel less comfortable around him. I felt less attracted to him. When we had sex, I couldn't shake the images of him with other women. He started to notice that I was less passionate. He noticed my voice was less soft. He didn't say anything, but I could see it on his face. He seemed hurt and confused.

One day, we were having dinner in a restaurant and I accused him of looking at other women. He denied it and asked me why I was so distant lately. I couldn't answer. I told him I didn't know.

That night, I seriously thought about leaving him. I felt like the whole relationship was falling apart. I tossed and turned all night. I asked myself why I was more distant. At five o'clock in the morning, it hit me like a ton of bricks: The reason I was feeling distant from Stu was because my mother was brainwashing me. She was undermining my ability to trust him even though there was no evidence he was doing anything wrong.

Once I realized this, my intimate feelings toward Stu returned. They were even stronger. I had almost left him. That would have *been the biggest mistake of my life. He is a wonderful husband and the love of my life.*

My mother still speaks poorly of Stu, but it no longer affects me or my marriage. All it does is make me want to spend less time with her.

Healing Damaged Relationships

Delilah was able to halt the process of her mother separating her from Stu before significant damage was done to their relationship. If you grew up with a parent with significant symptoms of BPD, there are probably many relationships that were damaged over the years.

Siblings, cousins, grandparents, neighbors, and others who your parent comes to perceive as threatening may be added to the list of personas non grata. Your parent considered it a betrayal for you to associate with these individuals. It is not uncommon for parents with BPD to fabricate stories about those they are threatened by. These stories are sometimes accusations of abuse or mistreatment.

One of the most destructive, but common, forms of alienation occurs in the context of divorce. Parents with symptoms of BPD are often very threatened by divorce and fear that their former spouse will try to take their children away from them. If successful, parental alienation can occur, where the child's relationship is damaged by the persistent denigration of the other parent. It is also common that groups of people may be treated as a threat and spoken about poorly.

Where divorce occurs, the parent may attempt to alienate the child from the entire family of the other parent. If you are the child of a divorced parent with symptoms of BPD and you are estranged from half of your family, you will likely benefit from reprocessing these relationships. Once you have stopped trusting untrustworthy people, you need to challenge your perceptions of who your estranged relatives and friends actually are. What they would look like in an accurate mirror.

You do this by examining the objective, subjective, and projective views of these individuals.

Examination of the objective view requires that you compare what you think about these people and your image of them. For example, if your parent told you that Uncle Harry was mean and abusive to others, you review your own experience. Did you ever see Uncle Harry being mean? Was he ever mean to you? You also can consult others who know Uncle Harry and ask them if Uncle Harry has a temper. You can also examine other factual evidence. For example, does Uncle Harry have many friends? How do others speak about him? Is he successful?

The projective view is clear: your parent is projecting negativity and a negative toward people they do not want you to have a relationship with.

The subjective view may not be as clear. As you can see in the example with Delilah, her mother's projected negative images of Stu were becoming harder to distinguish from her own experiences. She was starting to see what her mother was suggesting rather than what was actually occurring. Stu was not manifesting disloyal behavior, but Delilah was feeling as though he was.

This dissonance is where emotional reprocessing is applied. Delilah must focus on how her feelings about Stu were what her mother wanted her to feel, not a reaction to his actual treatment of her.

As you endeavor to do this with relatives and friends who were left behind, you will remember more experiences you had with these individuals. The projected negative images of the parent on a child often result in the child suppressing memories of events that disconfirmed the parent's images. It was not safe to entertain those images because your parent considered that a betrayal and probably punished you for it. This process can be facilitated by direct inquiry. For example, Delilah can ask herself if she recalls any instances of Stu going out of his way to make her feel safe, adored, honored, or respected.

Alienation of Social Groups

We looked at how a parent with symptoms of BPD often alienate their children from individuals and entire families. In the same manner, entire groups of people can be denigrated. Here are some examples:

> "You don't want to hang out with people from the city. They are aggressive and lawless."

> "All lawyers are out to take your money."

> "Pet owners are foolish."

> "People who like the Grateful Dead are drug addicts."

The process of emotional reprocessing can also be applied to groups. When children of parents with negative views of groups of people challenge that negative view with objective, subjective, and projective views, bias and bigotry can be diminished or eliminated.

In this chapter, you learned how to restart the growth of your social functioning and social networking. This will allow you to experience secure contextual relationships with those who are capable. It will also help you to function transactionally without getting hurt or taken advantage of by those who are not capable. I also showed you how to apply the process of emotional reprocessing to reclaim damaged relationships.

In the next chapter, you will learn how to guide your future growth. You will learn how to protect your growth from the projective influences of others who want you to be what they want you to be. If you have spent your life reacting to others, people pleasing, or allowing others to define you, you may not even be aware that your personal development was co-opted. If so, you can look forward to a freedom that you never even dreamed of. The freedom to be you. But there is still a lot of work to be done.

Chapter 10

Consciously Creating Your Self Today

Children of parents who have significant symptoms of BPD often suffer sustained emotional trauma during their most formative years. If you grew up this way, it might have impacted your ability to develop a healthy personality. The process of developing a sense of self is often profoundly affected by being lied to and gaslighted by a primary parent. In the first nine chapters, you learned how your development was affected and how to correct the distortions of the broken mirror. In this chapter, you will learn how to guide your future growth and development in a way that is immune to the toxic influences you grew up with.

The Mirror Revisited

Healthy personal growth continues throughout your lifespan. Unhealthy parents, such as those with symptoms of BPD, often influence the development of their child's personality in ways that primarily benefit the parent. Ways that inhibit independence and focus on securing the child's loyalty and availability to serve the parent. This often involves reflecting distorted images through the broken mirror.

Common examples include persistent feedback that you are not good enough. Many of you were told throughout your childhood that you are ungrateful or that your parent wished you were never born. Your efforts to be a good son/daughter were labeled as not good enough. You were subject to constant criticism and discouraged from having any opinions or decisions that were not the same as your parent or in your parent's best interest. This persistent influence most likely eroded your self-esteem and your self-confidence. Your sense of self was affected by the distortions, lies, and gaslighting that was provided by your parent.

You must immediately neutralize the toxic effects of the broken mirror. I will show you how to do this while continuing to benefit from healthy mirroring. Here is how you can tell the difference between healthy uses of mirroring and the toxic effects of a broken mirror. We will begin by defining two different types of mirroring that commonly occur during childhood.

Direct Mirroring

Mirroring is a critical tool for learning beginning in infancy and continuing throughout your life. Direct mirroring involves observing a model and imitating that model in order to learn from others. This is a critical tool for learning most cognitive functions including language, social skills, academics, etc. Parents teach their children to speak by saying words slowly and encouraging their children to copy, or mirror, them. Motor learning is also facilitated by direct mirroring. Taking a golf or tennis lesson, for example, involves watching a pro swing a club or racket while you attempt to imitate. Direct mirroring is healthy as long as healthy behaviors are being modeled.

You need to investigate unhealthy behaviors and thinking patterns that you learned from your parent and eliminate the influences of those behaviors. I understand you consciously try not to emulate your parent's behaviors. You don't lash out at others. You don't threaten suicide to manipulate others into doing what you want them to do. You don't injure yourself when you are frustrated. Some of the patterns of thinking and behavior are probably affecting you in ways that you are not consciously aware of. To fully understand and eradicate these effects, you will need to simultaneously consider the influence of reflective mirroring and direct mirroring.

Reflective Mirroring

Parents use reflective mirroring to help children learn about themselves and develop healthy social skills. They give *accurate* feedback to their children so that they can develop the ability to accurately self-reflect. In this type of mirroring, the parent mirrors the child, in contrast to direct mirroring, when the child mirrors the parent. For example, healthy parents naturally begin parenting their children in infancy. When the infant smiles, the parent smiles back and the infant learns that smiling makes others happy. When the child expresses frustration, the parent mirrors back the distress, signaling that the child's expression has been heard.

As the child gets older, healthy parents use verbal feedback to enhance the mirroring process. Common examples of this type of mirroring include:

"You frightened your little sister."

"You made your grandfather very happy today."

"You seem unhappy about going to camp."

"You don't seem to care about your studies."

These reflections help the child learn to be interpersonally effective, more in touch with his or her feelings, and more invested in growth and achievement. The hope is that, by adulthood, the child will be able to self-reflect rather than be reliant on the feedback of others.

Parents with symptoms of BPD do not want you to learn to self-reflect. They want you to depend on them for guidance and instruction.

They project into the mirror what they want you to see, rather than reflect the truth. This is what creates the broken mirror.

Neutralizing the effects of the broken mirror requires that you identify distorted feedback and dismiss it. In chapters 7, 8, and 9, you learned how to use emotional reprocessing to reclaim aspects of yourself and your relationships negatively impacted by the broken mirror. I will show you how to prevent the effects of growing up with distorted parental feedback from contaminating your future personal growth.

Now that you have emotionally reprocessed the distortions of the past, you must examine distortions in the way you were taught to process new events and information. You need to examine the lens through which you see the world and evaluate your bias in the way you view the world. Here are a few common examples:

Protect the Sanctity of the Truth

The truth is the truth. It is not negotiable and must not be subject to manipulation. You grew up with a parent who discounts, disregards, and fabricates the truth. This is done with selective memory, lying, gaslighting, and making up stories that fit a narrative. If you want to control your personal growth and free yourself from the pain of your childhood, you must commit to never treating others this way.

Commit to not treating yourself this way. You must face the truth head-on. You cannot ignore or discount it. For example, if you make a mistake, own it and do not tell yourself a story that justifies a bad decision or damaging actions. You accept errors, make good on them, and then learn from the experience. Giving yourself the opportunity to learn from errors is necessary to maximize your personal growth. You accept your limitations and learn from them rather than hiding them and pretending they don't exist.

Also, commit to emotional honesty. Lies of omission are lies, just like any other. Don't justify doing things that are bad for you. Don't pretend something doesn't bother you when it does. This is necessary to defeat the dissociation that was discussed in chapters 2 and 6 in detail and referred to elsewhere throughout this book. You may choose not to express these feelings to others, but you must be brutally honest with yourself about how you are affected by your physical and social environment. You don't pretend to like people or things that you find bothersome. You may decide to maintain relationships or participate in activities that you don't like, but you only do so for commensurate benefit.

Develop the Ability to Trust Again

A very common symptom of BPD is transient paranoid thinking. This causes individuals with symptoms of BPD to be generally distrustful of others. It is very common for parents with symptoms of BPD to directly mirror persistent distrust of others for their children. Your parent probably shared with you their thoughts about not trusting friends, relatives, coworkers, and neighbors. This is especially true when these individuals disagree with or displease your parent. Your parent also may have encouraged you not to trust friends, or groups of people your parent is unhappy with.

Ask yourself, *Why don't I trust people?* Do you have specific memories of betrayal or disappointment that would support your expectations, or are you just experiencing your parent's way of looking at the world? You were raised to believe that your parent's way of looking at the world is "normal," so you might never have questioned it.

As you question, use the emotional processing tools you learned in chapter 7. Examine the development of your bias toward distrust from the three different perspectives: objective, subjective, and projective. What actually happened, how it seemed to you at the time, and what others wanted you to experience. Now you can decide how you feel about trusting others from an independent adult perspective. Pearl's journey illustrates this.

Pearl's Story

Pearl is a thirty-five-year-old professional woman who struggles with intimate relationships. She is very attractive and interesting to talk to, so she has no trouble attracting interest from other single people. She just got out of a relationship and wrote down the following reflections.

"Here I go again. I blew another relationship. As soon as I get close to someone, I start to get anxious. The closer I get, the more uncomfortable I get. Eventually, I sabotage the relationship to get relief. I feel like such a fool.

Why am I afraid of men? Why do I always feel like they are taking advantage of me or planning to do so?

What have men done to me that has caused such a deep fear? I couldn't come up with a single memory of a man hurting me or threatening me. When did I start feeling this way? I always remember feeling this way. I did not feel comfortable around my father or grandfather. I am so afraid of male doctors that I can only see females, even when there are male doctors who are better trained or more available.

Then I remembered my mother telling me over and over again not to trust **ANY** man for **ANYTHING**! She often told me that they would take advantage of me sexually and financially. She told me that they would get drunk and beat me.

When I was a little girl, I asked her, "What about Daddy? He's a man. You trust him, don't you?" I was shocked when she answered, 'Especially him.' Daddy always made me feel safe and comfortable. If I can't trust him, how could I ever trust any man?

All at once, I realized that my fear of men was actually my mother's fear of men. I had no reason to be afraid of men. I had no experiences to support those feelings. Upon further reflection, my mother did not act like someone who was afraid of men herself. She married my father and had no trouble working or socializing* *with men. My fear of men was what my mother wanted me to feel so that I would always be available to her. These are not my feelings even though until now they felt just like they were."*

Pearl was craving intimacy in her life, but was unable to trust a man enough to sustain relationships beyond a certain point of intimacy. She wanted to direct her personal growth toward becoming a more trusting person. She explored her fear of men and came to realize that she did not have a natural fear of men but rather she developed this fear associated with her mother's use of the broken mirror, which inhibited her growth in the area of adult intimacy.

Recognizing this set her free to explore trust and intimacy on her own terms and not be saddled by a fear that was projected by her mother through the broken mirror. The anxiety did not go away all at once. She had to take some risks, like letting a man spend the night in her apartment or sharing feelings and thoughts that she is not proud of, to discover that there are people who will honor her and treat her with respect. It will also give her the chance to choose men who are safe and to gain confidence in her ability to make those judgments.

Truth and trust are just two common examples of attitudes and biases that were likely projected onto you by your parent and through the broken mirror. You need to examine all of them. Other common areas of projected bias include attitudes about money, justice, generosity, following rules, and respecting authority. The more you look, the more you will find. Then it will be time to outgrow the mirror.

Outgrow the Mirror

Having confidence in your ability to self-reflect largely mitigates the need to have others show you or tell you how you appear to others. You should still choose direct mirroring for the purpose of skill acquisition. There is nothing unhealthy about using mirroring as a way to improve your golf swing or become a yoga instructor or portfolio manager. You should not rely on the perceptions or opinions of others as part of your personal growth.

Many parents with symptoms of BPD encourage their children to become dependent on them by teaching them to trust the opinions, perceptions, and judgments of others over their own. This makes you dependent on the mirror and the feedback of others. This needs to stop immediately. You don't need to be told you could have been nicer to someone or that you are not putting your full effort into something. You learn this through self-reflection and internal validation.

Unencumbered personal growth requires that you replace external validation, which you get from others, with internal validation, which you provide for yourself. You must stop looking to others to tell you that you are a good person. You decide if you are a good person. You know better than anyone what you do, what you don't do, and what your intentions are. You don't need others to tell you if you did a good job or performed well at work or in other pursuits. You don't need others to tell you that you are generous or kind.

Most importantly, you do not need others to validate your self-worth. When you allow others to define your self-worth, you allow others to define you: your personality. You become who they want you to be rather than who you want to be. It is your time to outgrow this. If you have made significant progress in the path described here toward healing and growth, then you deserve to graduate from the binds of being steered by others. You must free yourself to maximize your gains in personal growth to be the best you can be.

Grow Free from Tethers: How to Take Control of Your Future Development

Once you free yourself from the projected opinions, attitudes, and directives for you, you can truly be the master of your self-development. Rather than becoming the person that others want you to be, you can be the you that makes you feel most proud, most satisfied, most fulfilled with being you. In the example above, Pearl was raised to not trust others, especially men. Once she understood that this perspective came from her mother's experience and conceptualization, and not hers, she decided that she wanted to become a person more capable of trust. She then created a strategy to mature in this direction.

Enhance the aspects of your personality by looking for opportunities in your daily life to express these traits. The purpose of increasing the expression of these traits is to make them a part of your life and yourself, not to satisfy others. For example, if you choose to be a more generous person, you look for opportunities in your life to give to others. You pursue giving in ways that are most meaningful to you. The more that you give to others, the more like a generous person you will feel. As generosity becomes habitual, you will become a more generous person.

You allow yourself to define what honesty is to you. You might decide it is most important to you to express generosity by offering your time or your sympathies rather than giving money or material goods.

You might choose to be a truthful person. You attain this by focusing on opportunities to express your honesty. You unfailingly tell the truth to yourself and others. You define for yourself what a more honest person looks like and you act that way every time you have the opportunity to do so. For example, you may decide that it is honest to tell people that you are not comfortable offering your opinions or recollections in certain circumstances.

Using this method of self-directed growth is the only way you can maximize personal growth. It is probably not the way you were raised to approach growth and independence. Parents with symptoms of BPD often encourage their children in the opposite direction. These parents want their children to follow the parent's direction rather than focus on their own. They fear their child's independence and tend to avoid supporting it. Nothing is limiting your personal growth except you. You can choose to be a more productive, thoughtful, generous, assertive, or loyal person and make it happen. You define yourself in your idealized image and pursue being that person.

If your parent is still alive, they will probably not be pleased by your efforts to maximize your growth and independence. To fully benefit from all of the effort you put in to heal from the lingering effects of childhood trauma, you must commit that you will no longer put the feelings and needs of people ahead of yours who do not do the same for you. A parent who intentionally or unintentionally inhibits your growth and discourages your independence is such a parent.

Your parent also may accuse you of abandoning them because you are no longer allowing them to define your relationship with them. You can explain to them that you are available to them, but that you expect those that claim to love you to be supportive of your healing and growth. Your parent may not be able or willing to understand this, but it might be worth a try or two. Beyond that, it is up to them to understand you, or choose not to and accept the diminished closeness.

Whether your parent is still alive or not, you will benefit from decreasing your sensitivity to others being displeased with your choices. You were probably trained to be very sensitive to whether or not others were pleased. You might have been punished for not pleasing your parent with symptoms of BPD. Whether or not others are pleased by you is up to them. Healthy relationships are based on accepting others for who they are.

Looking to others to define you or tell you that you are a good person, a generous person, or an honest person is likely to be retraumatizing to you and a significant setback. You would be once again trusting the opinions of others over your own opinions, judgments, and perceptions. This will tear down the self-confidence and self-esteem you have built up and it makes you vulnerable to someone setting up a broken mirror for their own purposes. While you can consider the opinions of others, your primary source of validation needs to be you. You must learn to trust yourself above others unless you have reason to believe that you are impaired. Examples of such impairment would be an addiction or some sort of compromise in your cognitive ability.

Becoming a Confident Self-Validator

To maximize your self guided personal growth, you will need to safeguard the process from the intrusive influences of others. Reliance on your ability to validate yourself will serve you well. Remember: You create your own mirror by using honest self-reflection. Over time and with experience, you will develop a method of self-reflection that works best for you that you can use with confidence.

As a starting point, I suggest you adapt your tools for emotional processing and reprocessing to self-reflection. I will show you how to validate yourself using objective, subjective, and projective views of yourself. For example, let's say you have been working hard on being a more generous person. Growth processes require frequent feedback as to whether your efforts are effective. So, you begin by reflecting on the objective view. Here are some questions you might ask yourself:

Objective Questions

- What have I done in the last three months to be a more generous person?

- Am I putting in more effort to be generous?

- Am I doing the most I can do? If not, why not?

- What opportunities to be more generous have I let pass in the last three months?

Who could answer these questions about you, better than you? You don't need others to validate your objective view of yourself. You just need to be honest with yourself. This is even more clear with your subjective view of yourself. Here are a few sample questions you might ask yourself to support your introspection:

Subjective Questions

- Do I feel different as a result of my efforts to be a more generous person?

- Do I feel like a more generous person?

- Do I feel more respectful of myself?

- Do I feel better about myself?

- Do I feel better about my life?

The answer to these questions provides valuable information to you in your efforts to direct your personal development in directions that enhance those aspects of yourself you consider most important. Only you know how you feel. Any feedback you get from others about how you feel is by definition inferior to your own self-reflections and therefore of little or no value.

The third view that you examine for the purpose of self-validation is the most complex, but also the most informative. Adaptation of your processing tools for use in self-validation requires that you examine your own projections. This largely involves your expectations and wishes of who you are and who you want to be. For example, people who suffer from low confidence or low self-esteem very often expect and therefore project failure onto new endeavors. They expect themselves to fail and feel like they are failures before embarking on a new challenge.

One major benefit of examining your own projections is that it guides you in differentiating what you expect to happen from what is actually happening. People who project failure onto themselves feel like they are failing even when they are succeeding. This can cause them to act like they are failing, such as by reducing effort or apologizing to others. This often causes failure where success is likely or imminent. Here are some examples of questions that you might ask yourself to aid in the examination of your projections:

Projective Questions

- What do I think it will be like to be a more generous person?

- What do I think it will take to make this happen?

- How do I expect to feel?

- How do I think my life will be impacted by success?

- How do I think my life will be impacted by failure?

Other people can only get access to this information if you give it to them. The best they can do is give back to you what you already shared with them. This has no additive value. Distortions in their recollections of what you shared with them function as a broken mirror. It reflects distorted or tainted information rather than the pure truth, which you already have access to.

Self-examination of projections offers the opportunity not only to understand your projections about a particular topic, such as becoming more generous, but also to reveal how you approach challenges in general. If you are a person who projects failure onto new endeavors, you can use this understanding to prevent self-sabotage by projecting failure. You can prepare to feel like you are failing, even when you are not, and commit to lifting your efforts when you experience this feeling, rather than letting things fall apart.

Healing Is a Process, Not an Event

You picked up this book because you knew that something in yourself and your life was wrong. You probably suspected that it had something to do with being raised by a parent with mental health issues, but you couldn't quite put your finger on it. In this volume, you probably learned that your parent is sicker than you thought and that their impact on your development was greater than you imagined. You came to understand that by normalizing aspects of your childhood that were not normal, types of childhood damage became hidden from you.

You learned that some of the damage was traumatic. These traumatic experiences that forced you to live in the past are associated with intrusive traumatic recollections and dissociation. You also learned that your personal growth was probably interrupted and inhibited in some critical ways.

Preventing growth keeps you in the past and present. Neutralizing a lifetime of traumatic and persistent growth-inhibiting forces takes persistent effort and a lot of time to heal. It does not happen all at once. Be patient. You will see incremental benefit as you follow the path I outlined for you toward healing past wounds and future growth.

I have shared with you the process of emotional reprocessing and how to adapt this process to heal the past and give you control of your future growth directions. Using this process to become a competent and confident self-validator is your key to the future. It allows you to shed your past hurts and prevents you from getting stuck in the present and unable to grow. There is no limitation to how much you can grow. Make this a priority and you will change your life. You will stop being a trauma victim and start being a trauma survivor. You will finally experience peace of mind and there will be no turning back.

You deserve it.

Acknowledgments

I would like to thank the entire editorial staff at New Harbinger Publications for their support and encouragement. In particular, I would like to thank Georgia Kolias, my acquisition editor, for her tireless encouragement and support. I would like thank Diedre Hammons for the splendid copyediting. I would also like to thank Julie Bennett and Vicraj Gill for their help, support, and leadership.

I would like to thank Randi Kreger, who has shared her ideas, experience, and expertise in the interest of helping those affected by borderline personality disorder. I am honored and grateful for her taking the time to write the foreword for this volume.

I would also like to thank Frank Pollaro, who generously shared his perspective and support with me as I prepared this manuscript. His feedback was invaluable to this product.

Daniel S. Lobel, PhD, is a clinical psychologist who practices in Katonah, NY. He is an internationally known expert on borderline personality disorder (BPD), and consults with families all over the world who suffer with this disorder. He has taught at Mount Sinai School of Medicine, State University of New York, Hofstra School of Law, and lectures with the National Alliance on Mental Illness (NAMI). He has written four books on the topic of BPD, and also writes a blog on the *Psychology Today* website. He is author of *When a Loved One Has Borderline Personality Disorder*, *When Your Mother Has Borderline Personality Disorder*, and *When Your Daughter Has BPD*.

Real change *is* possible

For more than fifty years, New Harbinger has published
proven-effective self-help books and pioneering
workbooks to help readers of all ages and backgrounds
improve mental health and well-being, and achieve lasting
personal growth. In addition, our spirituality books
offer profound guidance for deepening awareness and
cultivating healing, self-discovery, and fulfillment.

Founded by psychologist Matthew McKay and
Patrick Fanning, New Harbinger is proud to be
an independent, employee-owned company.
Our books reflect our core values of integrity, innovation,
commitment, sustainability, compassion, and trust.
Written by leaders in the field and recommended by
therapists worldwide, New Harbinger books are practical,
accessible, and provide real tools for real change.

 **newharbinger**publications

MORE BOOKS from
NEW HARBINGER PUBLICATIONS

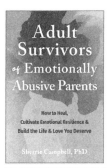